Presented to:

_____

From:

_____

Date:

_____

what my dog
has taught me about life

meditations for dog lovers

BY
GARY STANLEY

HONOR **HB** BOOKS

Inspiration and Motivation for the Seasons of Life

COOK COMMUNICATIONS MINISTRIES
Colorado Springs, Colorado • Paris, Ontario
KINGSWAY COMMUNICATIONS LTD
Eastbourne, England

Honor Books® is an imprint of
Cook Communications Ministries, Colorado Springs, CO 80918
Cook Communications, Paris, Ontario
Kingsway Communications, Eastbourne, England

What My Dog Has Taught Me about Life: Meditations for Dog Lovers
© 1999, 2007 Gary Stanley

Designed by Diane Whisner in association with Bordon Books, Tulsa, OK
Interior photos: ©Digitalvision/Inmagine.com,
          ©Stockbyte/Getty Images,
          ©Dex Image/Getty Images,
          ©Istockphoto
          ©Photodisc/Getty Images
          ©Digital Vision/Getty Images

First Printing, 2007
Printed in Canada

1 2 3 4 5 6 7 8 9 10

ISBN 978-1-56292-941-1

To Waddles, George, and Griffin for thirty-six years of love, lessons, and licks.

Acknowledgments

This has been a good year for the Plot and Blot Society! Alan, Ray, and Kirsten, thank you for editing my ideas, encouraging my thoughts, and contributing to all of our dreams. And Janet, you watch over us all and champion for us in the mysterious world of publishing. Who could ask for better friends?

To my fellow dog lovers, thank you for sharing your pets with me, and often so much more. Here they are—the stories where our lives intersected through the wag of a tail, a howl in the night, or a walk in the park. So, to Mom and Dad, Aunt Judy and Uncle Fred, Aunt Gloria and Uncle Wig, Bonnie and Van, Alma Dell and Jeff, Mike, Lee, Dub, Randy, Tom, Connie, Ryan, Jason, Terry Jo, Megan, Chris, the Scripps Cul-de-sac gang, Nathan, the Schoenlebers, Ann Reynolds, Tammy and Joe, my friends at the Northside Veterinarian Clinic, and the folks at Guide Dogs of the Desert—thank you!

To Luci, who always reads what I write with a much larger audience of One in mind, your fingerprints are all over this book as well as my life. Where would I be without you? Thank you, dear heart. Who knows, we might just get that Jacuzzi yet!

Contents

Foreword

Take a simple story about a dog, wrap it around the human heart, and thread it into God's grand narrative. If you do, you'll have something close to what awaits you in *What My Dog Has Taught Me about Life*.

In my lifetime, I have enjoyed the company of six dogs, a couple of cats, three horses, a donkey who thought he was a dog, a goat, a bilingual myna bird, assorted goldfish and guppies, an occasional parakeet, a circus chameleon, and one nocturnal hermit crab.

Some of these pets hardly touched my life at all, but most of them marked my life in ways I'll never forget—especially the dogs. Every one of them had a unique personality that forced me to revise and add to my theories about the nature of love, life, God, and reality.

As I introduce you to each one of my faithful friends, I hope you'll find yourself remembering the antics of your own dogs and what they taught you about life.

Gary Stanley

Working Vocabularies

Thirty-Word Dog

A few years back, one of the professors at the school where I taught proclaimed that Nathan, her two-year-old, had a working vocabulary of twenty-five words. I wasn't quite sure how I was supposed to respond. It was certainly a novel thing to note—so precise and definitive—a celebration of some sort of verbal benchmark. She seemed quite pleased, so I smiled and noted that she and her husband did indeed have a bright boy.

That night I checked out Griffin's working vocabulary—it was thirty words. Griffin is a year or two older than Nathan, but I figured I was in possession of a remarkable bit of news. Probably should have kept it to myself. Probably should have just let it slide—didn't.

At the first opportunity, I informed my colleague that Griffin's vocabulary was thirty words. I think I caught her a bit by surprise. She knows Griffin, and after a moment's reflection she congratulated me on that remarkable accomplishment and changed the subject. I felt a bit

Something to ● Chew on

When making comparisons, remember that someone always comes out with the short stick, and not everyone wants to play catch with it.

uneasy after our conversation, sensing that I'd stepped over some invisible boundary seen only by parents of actual children.

That little boy is now in the third grade, and his working vocabulary is well beyond numbering—he is indeed a bright boy. Griffin, on the other hand, is still in possession of the same thirty-word vocabulary. Turns out he's pretty smart too—for a dog. He's even done a couple of bit parts for Disney, playing Old Yeller.

At this point, let me ease any parental discomfort you may be experiencing. I know a dog is not a child. The theological reality is that one has a spirit and the other doesn't. One is an image-bearer of the Creator, and the other merely a reflection. One has eternity set in his or her heart, and the other has only a vague ache it shares with all creation. Still, the working vocabularies of life can be gleaned both from those who crawl on all fours as well as those who walk on all fours.

● ● ● ● ● ● ● ● ● ● ● ● ● ● ●

Paws **for** Prayer

*Father, remind me that my true significance
is never found in comparing myself to
others. Amen.*

Let not the wise man boast

of his wisdom.… But let

him who boasts boast about

this: that he understands

and knows me.

Jeremiah 9:23–24 NIV

Mutterings

The difference between
children and puppies is that
children grow up.

—W. C. Fields

The Best Laid Plans of Boys and Jackrabbits

The Tale of the Texas Jackrabbit

Every family has them. They are impossible to escape, often embarrassing, seldom new, and usually greeted with, "Come on! Not that again!" You can't really be a family without them—you wouldn't want to be. It is the narrative thread that defines a collection of folks as family, a special blend of stories and observations that shapes and secures your place in this world. It is likely the most potent thing we pass from one generation to the next.

Next time you're at a family gathering, just listen. It won't be long before someone is reminded of a well-worn story that everyone knows by heart. That's the thing about family narratives—we know them by heart, because that's where we keep them.

I can't think about my dad for long without picturing him spinning one of his tales about growing up in the Texas Panhandle. He lived in an era of small towns and wide open spaces. He had a big old bloodhound named Carlos that loved two things—keeping him company and chasing jackrabbits.

Now despite all the tales about Texas whoppers, a healthy jackrabbit can top thirty pounds and hit thirty miles an hour with

The Tale of the Texas Jackrabbit

■ ■ ■ ■ ■ ■ ■ ■ ■ ■ ■ ■ ■ ■ ■

great regularity. They can also run circles around most hounds.

One day Dad's dog was hot on the trail of a Texas-size jack when both of them disappeared into one of the many draws that crisscross the high plains. Dad knew that particular draw curved back on itself right next to where he was standing. So he figured he'd just drop down into that narrow gully and catch himself a rabbit. He hunkered down, coiling his nine-year-old frame, ready to spring. He could hear the sounds of the chase coming his way and could almost taste stewed jackrabbit as he waited on the other side of a blind corner.

The jackrabbit was running for all he was worth, drifting up the sandy sides of that miniature canyon with each twist and turn. He never saw my dad— didn't slow by so much as a whisker.

That jack hit Dad right in the stomach and proceeded to thump his head with both hind feet. It left him winded, sprawled, and semiconscious on the floor of the draw.

Dad was just beginning to appreciate how humiliating (and painful) it was to be run over by a rabbit when he heard the deep, throaty howl of his approaching hound echoing off the next bend in the draw. What happened next gave Dad a whole new appreciation of the phrase "roadkill."

Paws **for** Prayer

O Father, when I'm winded and flat on my back, remind me that this moment is not the whole story. Amen.

There is … a time to weep and a

time to laugh, a time to mourn

and a time to dance.

Ecclesiastes 3:1, 4 NIV

Mutterings

Experience is a hard
teacher because she gives
the test first, the
lesson afterwards.

—Vernon Law

The Donkey Who Thought He Was a Dog

Natural-Born Swimmer

Something to ◆ Chew on

Choose your models carefully, or you may find yourself trying to become something you were never intended to be.

When I was five years old, Dad brought home a Weimaraner puppy named Star. Of all the dogs we've ever had, the Weimaraner was the most ethereal. They are deerlike in appearance with green eyes and champagne-colored hair. The first time I saw Star, I wanted to know what happened to his tail.

"Cut off," Dad said.

"Why?"

"A Weimaraner just wouldn't look right with a tail."

It didn't look like there would be any better answer in the offing, so I dropped it.

"Look at his feet," Dad beamed. "They're webbed!"

Dad spread Star's toes, and sure enough, there was a lot of skin between those toes. "He's a natural-born swimmer." And that he was.

He was also the guiding light for our donkey. The donkey followed the dog everywhere and did everything the dog did. It is one thing to have a playful dog running around. It is quite another to have a playful donkey.

16

Natural-Born Swimmer

◆ ◆ ◆ ◆ ◆ ◆ ◆ ◆ ◆ ◆ ◆ ◆ ◆ ◆ ◆

When Star would grab a rag and shake it, the donkey would grab something more his size, like a blanket off the clothesline, to shake. When Star rolled in the dirt, the donkey joined him. When the dog snoozed on the front porch, so did the donkey (blocking all hope of using the door until naptime was over). When Star stood at the edge of the lake to bark at the geese, the donkey added his bray to Star's rebuke. But when Star would go for his daily swim, the donkey hung his head and dug in his heels.

Star was made for water. The donkey wasn't. Hooves are a poor substitute for webbed feet. Poor thing would stand on the shore and bray his heart out. Then one day we heard a big splash, and sure enough, there was the donkey swimming in the lake with Star.

I suppose we all model our lives after someone. Often it is just a matter of chance. We're thrown together with no real thought as to the long-term effect the relationship will have on us. Daddy always said, "You become like those you spend time with. Choose your friends well."

At first it was pretty funny watching that donkey trying to be a dog. After awhile, it became a problem. You

may be able to tolerate the smell of a wet dog, and Weimaraner dry quickly. But a donkey stays wet a long time and reeks, especially when he sleeps off his swim on the front porch.

Paws **for** Prayer

Lord God, may I live for an audience of One and not pander to the crowd. Amen.

Therefore be imitators of God, as beloved children.

Ephesians 5:1 RSV

Mutterings

Our soul is like wax.
Whatever we impress upon
it, it holds that image.

—Johann Arndt

Learning to Say Good-bye

Under the Apple Tree

Something to ♥ Chew on

A father's job is to help a child interpret life and put the hurts into a healthy place.

For six years, Waddles and I were inseparable—a boy and his dog. I can still remember the wonder that accompanied her one and only litter of pups, teaching her to jump through a hula hoop, racing across the fields near our house, and curling up with her next to a warm fire on a snowy night. The wag of her tail and sharp bark always welcomed me home—until one day in the spring of my twelfth year.

The last days of school were dragging by, and summer beckoned as I walked from the bus to the front door. Dad was there to meet me.

"I've got something hard we need to talk about," he said. "Waddles died this afternoon. She was playing next door, and our neighbor accidentally backed over her with his car." With that he enfolded me in his giant arms, and we cried.

He'd already prepared a small wooden box and dug a grave under one of the apple trees in the backyard. Together we placed Waddles into the ground, filled in the grave, and started to deal with the hole in our hearts.

20

Under the Apple Tree

I don't remember the exact words we shared that afternoon. But I do remember bits and pieces of the wisdom my father spoke as he helped me to place death in its proper context: "Everything we have is on loan from God." "Tears are an important part of life." "Don't bury your heart in the grave of someone you love."

In a lifetime of father-son talks, that was the single best conversation we ever had. Little did we know that six months later I'd be standing at another graveside—my dad's—saying good-bye just the way he taught me.

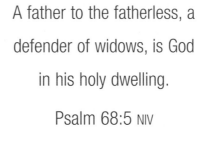

Paws **for** Prayer

Father God, remind me again that fatherless
living need never be. Amen.

A father to the fatherless, a

defender of widows, is God

in his holy dwelling.

Psalm 68:5 NIV

Mutterings

Death is not extinguishing
the light; it is putting
out the lamp because
dawn has come.

—Sir Rabindranath Tagore

Skippy

The Foo-Foo Dog

Images of Uncle Fred don't evoke words like *cute*, *perky*, or *dainty*. Uncle Fred was a carpenter. His world was a physical one full of manual labor, power tools, and half-finished projects. It showed in the calluses on his hands and the gruff expression on his unshaven face. He could put the fear of God into any little kid when he scowled down from his six-foot two-inch height.

The casual observer might match Uncle Fred with a junkyard dog. However, my Uncle Fred was partial to Schipperkes. A Schipperke is a cute, perky, long-haired little dog. A dainty dog. A pocket dog. A foo-foo dog.

Gruff on the outside, I figured Uncle Fred was hiding a soft heart inside. How else to explain Skippy, his Schipperke? Every morning Skippy accompanied Uncle Fred on his way to work, balanced lovingly on his shoulder.

As a boy, I'd sneak up on Uncle Fred and make him jump by tickling him in his side. He'd jump, scowl, and pretend he was going to hit me. "Why, I ought to raise a knot on your head," he'd shout. And then he'd chuckle, and I'd duck; the blow never delivered. We

Something to ● Chew on

Gruff exteriors and timid hearts often go together. Approach with love … but be ready to duck.

played that scene a thousand times over the years. I always knew there was a sweet old man inside that rough exterior. I could see it in the way he treated Skippy.

I suppose it's not always true. Some of us treat our dogs better than our kids—get closer to a pet than our parents. But some of us learn the art of loving others by practicing on God's lesser creatures. Uncle Fred was one of those.

He mellowed with age. His emotions weren't so closely guarded. Tears came more readily to that old face than ever touched the smooth skin of his youth. Fred grew in his ability to express love. It was probably one of the reasons God drew his heart to Skippy in the first place.

Paws for Prayer

Dear God, I lay down my own protective outer shell and choose to risk the hidden regions of my heart that long to love and be loved. Amen.

Perfect love casts out fear,

because fear involves

punishment, and the one

who fears is not perfected

in love.

1 John 4:18

Mutterings

Whoever said you can't buy
love has never owned a
puppy.

—Anonymous

JR

The Guardian Shepherd

I only had one dog I didn't really like. He looked a bit like a scrawny fox with a skinny tail. Didn't much like to be petted. Didn't much care for my company. Independent and hard to train, JR gave little back in the way of love.

It wasn't as if he'd had a hard childhood; I got him just after he was weaned. I treated him the same way I treated every dog I'd owned, but the fact was JR was an aggravating ankle-biter to the core.

The best thing about JR was his friend, the big shepherd, who lived down the street. The shepherd was everything JR wasn't—big and beautiful, fun-loving and affectionate. What he saw in JR was beyond me, but the two of them were inseparable.

On JR's six-month birthday, I took him in for his final series of shots. He went to the vet mad and came home the same way.

Later that day he wandered off with the big shepherd, still nursing a grudge. Evening came, and there was still no sign of JR. I called … not that he ever came. I looked all over the neighborhood—no sign of him or the shepherd anywhere.

A neighbor came home just before dusk. He said he had just driven

Something to ■ Chew on

It's easy to love the lovable, but it doesn't do much for one's soul.

28

past a very tender moment out on Arapahoe Road. A big dog was standing guard over the body of a little dog that had apparently been run over.
Cars were having to dodge both of them.

That road was a couple of miles from our house, much too far for JR
to have wandered. Still, it was just possible.

Mom drove me over to have a look, and sure enough, at the bottom
of Arapahoe Hill was the big shepherd standing over JR's broken body.

There's a difference between consolable and inconsolable losses.
Consolable losses are the kind you eventually get over. Inconsolable
losses are the kind you learn to live with. Lose your car keys, and
although it may be inconvenient, you get over it. Lose an arm, and you
never just "get over it."

We buried JR in the same backyard where we'd buried
Waddles. I really felt bad that I didn't feel all that bad. *It
figures JR would wait to get run over until after I'd spent all
that money for his shots.* It was definitely an unworthy
thought, but definitely a consolable loss.

I imagine the big shepherd saw JR's death differently. I
lost a little vet money. He lost a companion. JR had one
true friend in this world—someone to stand guard when
he was down, to miss him when he was gone. Maybe that's
all it takes for an inconsolable bond to form. You can't really
compare humans and hounds on this level, but I can't help but

think I was the real loser that day. I suspect it is in loving, when there's little reason to think it will ever be returned, that shallow hearts are transformed into hearts deep enough to have inconsolable hurts.

Paws **for** Prayer

Father, purge me of the smallness of my heart that justifies loving only those who love me well in return. Amen.

But love your enemies, and do good, and lend, expecting nothing in return; and your reward will be great, and you will be sons of the Most High; for he is kind to the ungrateful and the selfish.

Luke 6:35 RSV

30

Mutterings

Relationships are like algebra; if you change your side of the equation, the other side changes as well.

—Abraham Argun

Things That Go Bump in the Night

The Spoiled Morning Snuggle

Something to ◆ Chew on

There's nobility in getting up and trying again when you fall down, but it works ever so much better if you look where you're going.

Intentionally creating a miniature Chihuahua is a bit like splitting the atom—you're never quite sure what you're going to get. Buttercup had an oversized cranium transported on an extremely tiny body. If you've ever seen Brain from the cartoon show *Pinky and the Brain*, you have a pretty good idea what Buttercup looked like—99 percent head and destined never to grow up. A pocket dog for life.

When you're that small, you need a lot of assistance. Every morning, my uncle Wig would awake to the sounds of Baby (Buttercup's mom) and Buttercup trying to jump into bed. Baby would make it. Buttercup wouldn't. Half asleep, Wig would reach down and lift the vertically challenged Buttercup onto the bed. It was a routine firmly fixed in Buttercup's wee little brain.

However, Baby and Buttercup spent the majority of the night in another part of the house. It was only in the morning that they ran down the hallway and into Aunt Gloria and Uncle Wig's bedroom for a morning snuggle. That particular hallway had a door that was never closed, until the one night we were visiting.

The Spoiled Morning Snuggle

◆ ◆ ◆ ◆ ◆ ◆ ◆ ◆ ◆ ◆ ◆ ◆ ◆ ◆ ◆

Knock. It wasn't a loud noise—just enough to pull Uncle Wig to the edge of consciousness.

Then a long silence.

Knock. There it was again, a bit louder this time. It was worth investigating.

Uncle Wig put on his bathrobe and wandered down the hall to check out the source of the sound. Opening the hallway door, he found Baby standing there, blocked in her attempt to reach the bedroom. And next to her, the unconscious body of Buttercup, who apparently liked to run with her head down.

Running into an unexpected obstacle didn't deter her from making another attempt to reach her goal. Buttercup apparently knocked herself out on her second attempt to run down a darkened hallway that just had to be open.

She fully recovered from her self-inflicted trauma, although it is not all that easy to determine a loss of capacity in a creature with little capacity to start with.

The Spoiled Morning Snuggle

Paws for Prayer

O God, increase my longing to walk in your light and spare me the needless wounds I always inflict upon myself when I sneak around in the dark. Amen.

I guide you in the way of wisdom and lead you along straight paths. When you walk, your steps will not be hampered; when you run, you will not stumble.

Proverbs 4:11–12 NIV

Mutterings

Zeal alone is never enough. It must be matched with truth.

Clyde and the Telegram

That Dirty Dog!

Something to ♥ Chew on

Don't believe everything you read. The words can be clear, and the truth still obscured.

Lady and the Tramp they weren't. No romantic spaghetti dinners served by a singing waiter behind the local Italian restaurant. No moonlit walks staring into each other's eyes. Their love story was based in a more earthly reality:

WESTERN UNION

HAD CAESAREAN SECTION AT 4:30PM. WOULD YOU BELIEVE IT, YOU HAVE TWO SONS AND FOUR DAUGHTERS. SINCE WE ARE NOT LEGALLY MARRIED, THE DOCTOR HAS PROMISED TO KEEP IT FROM THE PRESS FOR NOW. AND YOU SAID YOU WERE STERILE, YOU DIRTY DOG. ALL SEVEN OF US ARE FINE.

YOUR LADY

The woman at Western Union who took the message didn't know what to think! All she could say was, "Poor thing! You mean he told her he was sterile? Well, he is a dog! Poor thing!"

Aunt Judy didn't have the heart to tell the sympathetic telegraph operator that Clyde—the father of six—was indeed a dog. And Lady was the family pet.

Clyde was a proper English rogue, smuggled into the United States by a bunch of Air Force conspirators to avoid six months of

♡ ♥ ♡ ♡ ♥ ♥ ♡ ♥ ♥ ♡ ♥ ♡ ♡ ♥ ♡

quarantine and eight hundred dollars in expenses. He was eighty pounds of mischief who chewed through floor mats and the neighborhood dogs with equal ease. Still, you couldn't help but love that old rascal.

Clyde had a way of getting under your skin and into your heart. Even the local dogcatcher had a grudging affection for Clyde, who always managed to get back to his own front porch before the law could net him. And no one loved that mutt more than my cousin Bonnie.

When Bonnie and her husband, Van, moved in next door to Aunt Judy and Uncle Fred, it was only a matter of time before Lady would succumb to Clyde's charms.

Clyde's interest in Lady was not appreciated by Aunt Judy. Another litter of pups she could do without. Besides, Lady was a little thing. And genetics being what they are, Lady's life would be endangered by the size of the pups she carried if Clyde was the pop.

None of that mattered in the least to Clyde. Guess you could say "love found a way," if you're not too picky about how you define love. Sure enough, Lady was too small to carry all those pups to term. Aunt Judy and Uncle Fred paid for Lady's c-section, long after

That Dirty Dog!

Clyde left town when Van and Bonnie were transferred to Las Vegas.
And Aunt Judy's telegram? Well, it has become a family keepsake, a tangible reminder of a lovable old rogue, a costly affair, and our family's sense of humor.

Paws for Prayer

Father God, may your heavenly laughter edit my words and thoughts when I'd rather feed the sentiment, "This isn't my problem because it wasn't my fault." Amen.

Let no unwholesome word proceed from your mouth, but only such a word as is good for edification according to the need of the moment, so that it will give grace to those who hear.

Ephesians 4:29

Mutterings

Real love edits the truth
without distorting it.

The Things We Do for Love

Great Friendship Knows No Bounds

Lawrence Kolberg once thought ethical behavior was produced by sound ethical reasoning. He challenged his students with moral conundrums to develop this ability. He later changed his mind, concluding that knowing what is right doesn't naturally lead to doing what is right. He discovered that right living required little ethical reflection; the key was a practiced ethic that had become almost instinctive.

Something to ● Chew on

A life of loving responses is built up over time.

Aunt Judy was a caring woman, a LPN, which basically meant she was a lower-level nurse. Her calling in life was to care for others. I can't remember how many times she thanked God for a poor sense of smell, because it made it easier for her to clean out hospital bedpans.

Aunt Judy lived life in the nitty-gritty. She was kind and caring. She never thought twice about getting her hands dirty. But one day she surprised even herself.

Lady was about fifteen years old at the time. The little dog was shuffling across the linoleum in the family room. Suddenly, she shuttered, dropped, and stopped breathing. Aunt Judy saw the whole thing, and a lifetime of reflex just took over. She cradled the lit-tle dog in her big hands and pumped Lady's chest. When that didn't work, she gave Lady CPR, the mouth-to-mouth kind. If you had to think about it, most likely you'd wait too long or decide you'd rather not. Aunt Judy didn't think. She acted. And Lady revived and lived another five years.

I still remember Judy telling that story, unconsciously wiping her lips with a paper napkin. Then she'd chuckle and I could almost see her as a young coquettish farm girl.

"My, my!" she exclaimed. "The disgusting things we do."

No, Aunt Judy, you're wrong. It can't really be disgusting when it is so clearly an act of love—love that's too compassionate to sit around weighing the possible consequences.

● ● ● ● ● ● ● ● ● ● ● ● ● ● ● ●

Paws **for** Prayer

O Father, replace my initial reactions, which usually fail the test of love, with seasoned responses of love. I'm tired of having to go back and repent the rot of my flesh's firstfruits. Amen.

Let love be without hypocrisy. Abhor

what is evil; cling to what is good.

Romans 12:9

Mutterings

If you have to think
about it, you probably
haven't been practicing it.

Lost

A One-Sided Game of Hide-and-Seek

He was the pick of the litter—a white puff of cotton with a pink nose and a wispy hint of tail. Barely weaned, he was on his way to our family in the back of Aunt Judy and Uncle Fred's car.

They stopped to do some repairs on an old wood-framed rental house they owned. There was no sense in leaving the pup in the car so they brought him in with them.

By the time they noticed the pup had wandered off, he could have been anywhere. He was lost.

Ever been lost? I have. In the mountains. Late afternoon. Ten years old. It slowly grips your heart and settles into your stomach. You're lost.

Dad was an Eagle Scout. Eagle Scouts know stuff. "If you ever get lost, take a deep breath and stay put. Let those searching come to you."

"What if no one knows I'm lost, Daddy?"

"Oh, you'll always be missed."

The pup was missed. You'd think it would be easy to find a white dog in a house with a dark wood floor and no furniture. It wasn't. They whistled. They clapped. They yelled. But the pup had no name yet, no special sound that perked his ears or called him home.

They thought he must have gotten out somehow, but the fenced yard

Something to ▪ Chew on

Being missed is wonderful, but being found is better.

44

was empty. Maybe he was in the crawl space under the house. Crawl spaces are great places to hide, and lousy places to search. Hot and dirty, Uncle Fred finally satisfied Aunt Judy that the pup wasn't under there.

The day was gone. They searched the tiny house one more time, not out of any real hope of finding the lost pup. There was nothing left to do but give up and get on with life.

As Uncle Fred closed up the house, he walked past the bathroom door and something caught the corner of his eye. A tiny movement tickled his conscious mind. He stood there puzzling it out. Then he saw.

"Jewel, come here! Take a look at this!"

"Oh, for heaven's sake!"

The pup (that would soon be named George), had found a nice cool spot behind the white toilet and splayed out on his belly. Only the tip of his nose and a bit of tail extended beyond the porcelain base. He was all but invisible. He was also moments from being locked inside a house that wouldn't be reopened for weeks. He was lost, and he didn't even know it. He had been found in the nick of time.

I was missed too. It wasn't long before I heard Dad holler my name as he crested a nearby ridge in search of me. It worked just like he said it would. I

■ ■ ■ ■ ■ ■ ■ ■ ■ ■ ■ ■ ■ ■

was a little scared and a lot lost, but I stayed put and Dad searched until he found me.

Lost is the common condition we all share. Take a look around. Do you know where you are? Do you know the way home? If not, take a deep breath. Stay put. You will be missed. Oh yes, you might want to holler every so often. It will remind you that you're lost and make you easier to find.

Paws **for** Prayer

Dear Finder of Lost Things, thank you for finding me. Thank you for not giving up when the search took you to unpleasant places. Amen.

For the Son of Man has

come to seek and to save

that which was lost.

Luke 19:10

Mutterings

No one is ever so lost
that he ceases to be
missed by the One who
loves him most.

Sleepless in Boulder

Lee's Midnight Shower

They say a towel-wrapped windup clock is a good mother substitute for a worried puppy during its first few nights away from the litter. "They" are often wrong.

George's nocturnal protests that first night were hard to ignore. A puppy knows the difference between a towel and a tummy, a mechanical thump and a mom's heart.

We'd put our six-week-old pup in the hall bathroom and prayed he'd soon go to sleep. He didn't. And neither did we.

The powers of observation often grow keener when sleep is withheld. Lying there in the dark can focus the mind. Ever notice that proximity and responsibility often go together? The closer you are to a problem, the more likely it is that you will feel obliged to deal with it.

George's lonesome lament echoed off the porcelain tiles, beneath the two-inch gap under the bathroom door. My room was at the end of the hall, directly across from Mom's. We were equally distanced from our sleepless pup. However, my cousin Lee was spending the night with us in the room directly across the hall from the bathroom.

Something to ◆ Chew on

There are times when it is better to face your responsibilities with your mouth shut.

48

Lee's Midnight Shower

◆ ◆ ◆ ◆ ◆ ◆ ◆ ◆ ◆ ◆ ◆ ◆ ◆ ◆ ◆

Mom and I hunkered down in our beds, reasonably certain that another visit to reassure our mournful pup would just reinforce his wakeful worry. Doubtless Lee started out with the same mind, but sometime after midnight, his need for sleep overcame his sense of discipline. Lee retrieved George from the bathroom and put him on the bed.

George was delighted with this arrangement. Human warmth! New territory to explore! Whereas Lee wanted to sleep, George wanted to play. Whereas Lee anticipated a warm, sleepy fur ball, what he got was a squirming puppy.

Nature boasts any number of razor-sharp points: the porcupine's quill, the sea urchin's spine, and the nettle's thorn to name a few. And somewhere near the top of the list are the baby teeth of a puppy applied to the soft tissue of a human ear. Lee made this remarkable discovery on the edge of consciousness, done in by a creature no bigger than his fist.

Lee yanked George away from his ear and rolled over on his back. He held George's tiny face between both thumbs so the little fellow was suspended directly above Lee's scowling countenance. Lee began to sternly lecture his pint-sized tormentor nose to nose.

"Now listen, George!"

Lee's Midnight Shower

That's as far as he got. Lee's tone of voice literally opened the floodgates of his wee little bedmate. You might say he was rudely interrupted. You might say … well, there's really no delicate way to put it.

Lee deposited George back into his box and took his second shower of the night—to wash off the residue of the first.

Paws for Prayer

O Father, may I not have to learn every lesson in life from firsthand experience. Amen.

A gentle answer turns away

wrath, but a harsh word

stirs up anger.

Proverbs 15:1

Mutterings

Some days you're the
dog, some days you're
the hydrant.

—Anonymous

The Case of the Soggy Doggy: Part One

Can't Keep Up

Something to ♥ Chew on

Just because there's nothing new under the sun doesn't mean you've checked out all the shadows.

The dog days of summer had settled over the old neighborhood like a fine layer of dust. I like summers. There's something about the super-heated air when it hits me after jumping into a closed car that makes me feel warm all over.

The old neighborhood was open turf, and no one much cared if you took a shortcut across their property, which is exactly what the local pack of dogs did until some starched shirt came up with a leash law.

This particular bunch was an indiscriminate mix of terriers, hounds, shepherds, and mutts that were more interested in finding a cool place to snooze than causing any serious trouble. Oh, there were the usual complaints about how they marked their turf. But beyond that, there was no real bone to pick. At least that's what I told myself when George started hanging out with his canine chums. It all seemed innocent enough. They came from good homes, and they all had their shots. But George was still pocket-sized, and this was a fast crowd.

Can't Keep Up

The first time George showed up at the back door soaked to the bone, I put it down to a youthful romp through some sprinkler. It would all wash off. Giving George a bath did us both good. I hosed him down, and he returned the favor by shaking most of the water back on me.

Once was novel. Twice was tolerable. But by the third wash day in a row, my good humor was wearing thin. We were moving from a bad hair day to an entire week.

That evening I sipped a soda and tried to sort it out. Where did George go for his daily dunking? Why was he the only dog who came home soaked?

Maybe George was at fault, and maybe he wasn't. Either way, he wasn't talking and neither was anybody else. I dropped off to Never Never Land, dreaming of how I would tail "the tails," so to speak.

The next morning when I let George out for the day, I gave him a brief head start and followed. There was little challenge keeping tabs on the pack of pooches, even though they spent plenty of time doubling back just to throw me off the scent.

A wire-haired terrier took the lead and quickened the pace. The others followed their leader of the moment. Maybe they'd spotted me, and maybe they hadn't. One thing was sure, I'd come too far to quit now.

All at once, I heard a soulful moan, a throaty wail—a

perfect counterpoint to a sax solo of "Harlem Nights," Mike Hammer's theme song. It was George all right. He couldn't keep up. His little puppy legs were long on heart but short on stride. George had given up, a despondent heap in the gutter of life. I've been there myself a couple of times. (To be continued …)

Paws for Prayer

Dear Father, may I never lose the wonder that there's more to life than meets the eye. Amen.

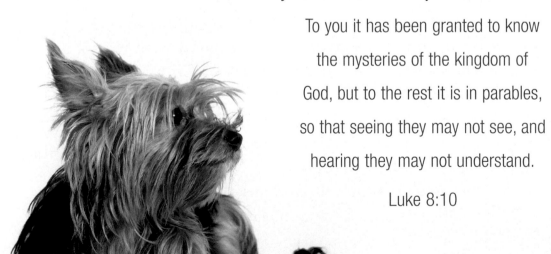

To you it has been granted to know the mysteries of the kingdom of God, but to the rest it is in parables, so that seeing they may not see, and hearing they may not understand.

Luke 8:10

Mutterings

When you have excluded the impossible, whatever remains, however improbable, must be the truth.

—Sherlock Holmes

The Case of the Soggy Doggy: Part Two

Free Ride

Life usually slaps you upside the head when you're not paying attention. That's why I like to keep up on my dues. But this time, she hit me square on the chops. I never saw it coming.

The big German shepherd was at least an eighty pounder. He had the confident gait of a top dog with nothing to prove. The moment George began his lament, the shepherd turned back. It was obvious the big dog was used to meeting trouble straight on. I figured George had about as much chance with this giant as Jack did without his beanstalk.

I stepped forward with no real plan in mind. If that long-toothed bruiser wanted a pound of flesh, I figured I was in a better position to donate a piece of flank steak than my three-pound pup. I steeled myself for the confrontation, when the big mutt suddenly lunged, scooping George up in his mouth like a tennis ball. Too late to prevent the inevitable, I froze waiting for the sound of his jaws snapping shut before he shook George and spit him out like a chewed-up toothpick.

George ceased his verbal complaints as he all but disappeared into the yawning abyss. But then I saw a sight that would make a grown man cry. That pitiful little wisp of a tail began to wag, and his little snout pushed out from under the big dog's lip a brave farewell reminiscent of a Coliseum Christian about to be devoured by a Roman lion. George was one prayer away from his Creator.

Call it what you like, we live in a notoriously unpredictable world. Appearances can still be deceiving, and motives aren't easily discerned. After picking up George, the shepherd trotted off to rejoin the other dogs, carrying his cargo as carefully as a mama cat carries her kittens.

When the pack slowed down again, George was carefully deposited onto the ground unharmed but covered with dog drool. The mystery was solved. I wasn't entirely comfortable with the shepherd's modus operandi, but hey, I'm as open-minded as the next guy.

Being able to quickly size up a person or a dog or a situation isn't optional in my line of work. Still, snap judgments have chipped more than one moral tooth.

We need someone who's willing to help carry us when the pace gets too fast and our legs can't keep up. And if the help musses our hair and leaves us wetter than we'd like? Well, I figure it's worth it.

Paws **for** Prayer

*Lord, free my timid heart to let you love me
in ways I don't really understand and would
never expect. Amen.*

Above all, keep fervent

in your love for one

another, because

love covers a

multitude of sins.

1 Peter 4:8

Mutterings

Tough love can
still be gentle.

The Last Time I Outran George

It Always Catches Up to You in the End

Oh, he could whine! Poor thing! Couldn't keep up. Hated to fall behind. Left in the dust. Deserted for all of five seconds. "Wo-wo-wo-wo-wo!" So unfair!

If you plan to outrun a dog, do it while he's young. You may be the leader of the pack for life, but odds are you won't be the sprint champ for long.

Once George was old enough to view life in relation to me, the race was on: around the outside of the house, circling the dividing wall between the slick kitchen floor and the carpeted living room, or just running flat out across a field. I reigned for just under six months, and then genetics defeated me—four legs run faster than two.

George's string of wins was broken only once. He was about two years old and in his prime. No longer did he suffer the indignity of being carried around in the mouth of the big shepherd. Summer was coming on, and the fields around our house were in high weeds.

Our sprints were spur-of-the-moment events—seasoned grudge matches, with a few false starts. I'd momentarily distract him, and then off I'd fly.

Something to ■ Chew on

The things that come back to bite you are often the things you got ahead of unfairly.

60

It Always Catches Up to You in the End

■ ■ ■ ■ ■ ■ ■ ■ ■ ■ ■ ■ ■ ■ ■ ■

The weed-infested slope from the upper road down to our street would let a long-legged runner cover twice the normal distance with each stride. What I was able to go over, George had to go through. It was just enough for me to pull ahead and hold my lead.

"Wo-wo-wo!" A painful pup memory had been accessed. An emotionally crippling handicap had been cruelly visited on the family speedster. Ha! No sympathy here! I hooted and hollered. Genetics were about to succumb to a botanical obstacle.

When I broke through the weeds and onto the gravel road, I was fifteen yards in the lead, and George's whimper was in full throat. I was only half a dozen steps from the garage and sure victory when the whimper stopped. I didn't dare look back to check how great or narrow my lead.

"Wo-wo-wo!" George's lament ceased and mine began. He bit me! My dog bit me! In the seat of the pants. Hard! My legs stopped while my mind tried to grasp what had happened. It just couldn't be. And George, my boon companion, faithful friend, and protector, having accomplished his purpose, raced into the garage.

Now that I think about it, I suppose George's string of wins was unbroken after all. Wish I could say the same about the skin on a sensitive part of my anatomy.

Paws **for Prayer**

O Lord, pace my heart that I may stay in step with you. I'm tired of running ahead only to later lag behind, exhausted and footsore. Amen.

If anyone competes as an athlete, he does not win the prize unless he competes according to the rules.

2 Timothy 2:5

Mutterings

All glory is fleeting,
especially if you had to
cheat to get it.

Grounded!

Biker Dog

First it was a riding lawn mower. Then it was a Honda 50 motorcycle with a floating clutch and 3.5 horsepower engine. Finally, it was a candy-apple red Yamaha Street Scrambler 250 with a five-port induction system and 30 horses. It could fly!

George and I survived my entire Yamaha phase with a minimum of scrapes and stitches. It started out innocently enough. George enjoyed running alongside my cycle, and he loved to ride in the car with his head stuck out the window chewing air.

One day it occurred to me that George would probably enjoy riding on the Yamaha with me—the wind in his face, the sense of power and speed. George would be a natural! He wasn't so sure.

The first time I put him on the seat, he wouldn't stay put and jumped right off. Eventually, I discovered that he'd consent to stay if he could brace himself by sitting in my lap with his front paws on the gas tank. After a few aborted attempts that ended before we'd reached the end of the driveway, we were off and running, leaning into every turn. It was a remarkable feat—a noteworthy accomplishment. I decided to keep it to myself. No need to test the bounds of parental permission.

Biker Dog

It wasn't long before George was jumping up on the motorcycle every time I got ready to ride. It also wasn't long before Mom began to notice this new behavior. Dogs have no sense of discretion. Still, it never occurred to Mom what was actually going on, and I saw no reason to broaden her horizons.

George and I became an item as we tooled around town. Folks would laugh and point us out to each other. At traffic lights, total strangers would roll down their windows to compliment us on our skill and daring. Girls began to notice! Life was good.

And then came the day Mom spotted us downtown on the Yamaha. Oops! She was not nearly as open-minded as I'd hoped. A perfect driving record carried no weight whatsoever. Grounded! Not me.

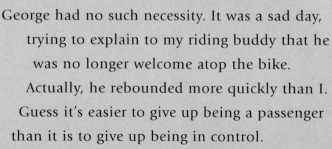

After all, I had to ride to my part-time job, but George had no such necessity. It was a sad day, trying to explain to my riding buddy that he was no longer welcome atop the bike.

Actually, he rebounded more quickly than I. Guess it's easier to give up being a passenger than it is to give up being in control.

Biker Dog

◆ ◆ ◆ ◆ ◆ ◆ ◆ ◆ ◆ ◆ ◆ ◆ ◆ ◆ ◆ ◆

Paws for Prayer

Father God, teach me to risk wisely, to sail farther from the shore, but keep a sharp eye on the compass. Amen.

All things are lawful, but not

all things are profitable.

1 Corinthians 10:23

Mutterings

Only those who will
risk going too far can
possibly find out how
far one can go.

—T. S. Eliot

Old Blue

The Bird Who Caught the Dog

George had to share his status as sole pet of the Stanley household only once when we were given a bilingual myna bird named Blue that was decades old.

If you've never owned a myna bird, there are a few things you might want to consider. Myna birds have a digestive track that goes straight from their mouth to their tail. Myna birds are loud and messy, solitary and mean. Mynas are also auditory marvels.

Bright and early every morning, Old Blue would rehearse his working vocabulary: "Hello, Blue," he'd say in his high voice.

"Hello, Blue," he'd say in his low voice.

"Ha, ha, ha, ha, ha!" he'd then crow.

"There's someone at the door. There's someone at the door," he'd say in his expectant voice.

"Caaugh, caaaugh, caaaaugh," sounded like an old man clearing his throat.

Then Blue would say something in Spanish, which we couldn't understand. A neighbor of ours, who used to teach Spanish, blushed the first time she heard Blue utter those infamous words and refused to translate them for us. We never did learn what it

Something to ♥ Chew on

The downside of the pecking order is seldom obvious until you lose your place to someone with a bigger beak.

68

meant although I suspect his name and his "blue" vocabulary were somehow connected.

Finally, Old Blue would give three loud wolf whistles.

The myna was confined to the atrium in the elaborate cage that came with him, while George spent much of his day outdoors. However, that all changed the day Blue started mimicking my whistle to call George.

Once Blue discovered that George was at his beck and call, George's life took a tortured turn. George would arrive at the atrium expecting to find me only to have Old Blue sit and laugh at him. "Ha. Ha. Ha." You'd think George would have soon ignored the whistle, but Blue was a great mimic, and George was trapped by years of conditioning.

When Blue lured George into the atrium, George would start to bark and jump up to nip at Blue's cage. Old Blue would sit there behind the close-spaced bars of his cage, turning his head from side to side, taunting George. Then, whop! Blue would peck George on the end of his nose with lightning speed. Annoyed and in pain, George would renew his attack only to suffer another bloody peck. It soon became obvious there would be no truce. It was either Old Blue or George.

We sold Old Blue to a local pet store. Within weeks, Blue's working vocabulary prompted a run on baby myna birds. I have no idea if any of the new birds they sold ever uttered a word, but I bet there was a rise in the number of bloody noses among the dog population.

Paws for Prayer

Dear Father, it's hard to be humble with ruffled feathers, and getting whopped seems to go with sticking my nose in the wrong place. I'd like to take this opportunity to renounce both activities. Amen.

Whoever wishes to become great

among you shall be your servant.

Mark 10:43

Mutterings

Never be haughty to the
humble. Never be humble
to the haughty.

—Jefferson Davis

$5 Puppies

The Matchmaker

Dub is one of those fellows who lives up to his name. It suits him—a blend of homespun common sense and humor. He was the perfect guy to help me through my rookie year as the director of a campus ministry in Louisiana.

When I was assigned to northern Louisiana, the only thing I knew about the region was what I'd read in the newspaper:

> Gator Gulps Down Dog
>
> MONROE, La. (UPI) Lester Shivers said he and a friend were training their dogs to retrieve a decoy Thursday evening when [a 14-foot] alligator surfaced behind Shivers' 65-pound dog and ate it in one bite.
>
> "There wasn't even any blood on the water," said Bob Hammack. "I yelled at my dog to come off the retrieve and when he didn't, I like a fool ran into the water and grabbed him and did a Louisiana two-step to get back on shore."

I envisioned alligators sunning themselves on the campus lawns, students sticking close to the sidewalks, and swamp moss hanging from the dormitory eaves. I dismissed any thoughts of taking George with me.

Something to ● Chew on

If you can't see the value in someone, you probably haven't dug pocket-deep and invested in them yet.

72

Dub helped me adapt to the culture and taught me a lot about working with people that year. He also had an uncommonly fine eye when it came to the dynamics of matching a litter of pups with their future owners.

The family pet's latest indiscretion had produced a litter of mongrel mutts—runts every one. Not a pick in the litter. Ugly as sin.

"These pups are way too ugly," said Dub. "We'll never be able to give 'em away. We're gonna have to sell 'em."

"Sell what you can't give away?"

"Yep. Have to sell 'em. Not for a dollar either. We'll have to insist on five dollars each." Seven weeks later, the pups were wide-eyed, weaned, and woefully lacking in the looks department.

Signs went up around the neighborhood:

PUPPIES FOR SALE—$5.

It wasn't long before a series of young boys were diggin' pocket-deep to purchase one of Dub's distinguished pups. Sold 'em all, every last one. I realized Dub wasn't getting rid of puppies through some slick advertising scheme or a bit of reverse psychology. He was publicly adding value to something with little obvious worth to the untrained

● ● ● ● ● ● ● ● ● ● ● ● ● ● ● ●

eye. A bunch of boys were each matched up with a pup too ugly not to love. I wonder if they ever knew?

I never did see any alligators or swamp moss during that year. If you're ever in the area, there's a pretty little campus just south of Interstate 20, and you'll probably find a whole lot of black and brown pups too ugly not to love.

Paws **for** Prayer

Father, I'm so easily influenced by the world's standards. Let me see the true value of a person or a thing through your eyes. Amen.

God sees not as man sees,

for man looks at the outward

appearance, but the LORD

looks at the heart.

1 Samuel 16:7

Mutterings

What we obtain too
cheap, we esteem
too lightly.

—Thomas Paine

Intruder Rabbit

The Dog versus the Hare

Something to ▪ Chew on

Forgiveness doesn't have to make sense but, oh, does it make a difference!

In his later years, George's domain was defined by a chain-link fence and challenged by the neighbor's "intruder rabbit." The rabbit's hutch was next to our common fence, and George spent much of his day keeping the rabbit company. They looked cute—pink nose to black nose through the galvanized wire openings. Tantalizingly close, they might as well have been on opposite sides of the Rocky Mountains.

They both faced the same moral dilemma—the fence. Fences define boundaries. Fences are authority figures just begging to be tested. Lay down a law, or a fence, and all of us immediately want to know how far we can push the limits.

One day, the rabbit mysteriously appeared in our backyard. It was high entertainment watching the two of them cut figure eights in the grass. The rabbit could turn on a dime. It cost George a quarter.

The general consensus was that George didn't stand a chance of laying a whisker on that hare. It became a matter of great pride for the two little girls who lived next door when I'd hand them back their rabbit over the fence. The reigning rabbit of the neighborhood was a part of their family.

The Dog versus the Hare

These sporadic contests went on for more than a year with little change. Then one day, George pranced around the far reaches of the backyard with what looked like a dirty rag. He high-stepped his way over to me and dropped his prize at my feet. The neighbor's rabbit had finally lost a race. It wasn't a game of tag after all.

Ethics are hard to apply to animals. The appearance of shame is usually a sham. Instinct shouldn't be confused for a conscience, but it often is. George suffered no regret for his actions. His lowered head and sagging tail had nothing to do with his moral dilemma; it merely reflected mine. "Bad dog!"

Bloody fur was washed and smoothed. A box was located for a casket. We broke the news to the parents of the little girls. A final resting place under the crab apple tree between our houses was prepared. The girls were told. They tasted death for the first time. They cried.

When you lose a pet, where do you place the loss? Where do you place the blame? For two little girls the world wasn't as safe as it had been a few hours earlier. A funeral is a good place to face life's uncertainties. No one knew how it would turn out. George faced the girls next to the crab apple tree as we buried the rabbit. Our morally blind dog did little to help his cause. He wagged his tail. Tried to be the center of attention. Sniffed around without a hint of

■ ■ ■ ■ ■ ■ ■ ■ ■ ■ ■ ■ ■ ■ ■ ■

remorse. And then the remarkable happened.

The two little girls hugged George around the neck and did what only humans can do—they forgave him.

Paws **for** Prayer

O Father God, remind me that nursing my hurt doesn't help, and forgiving doesn't mean they were right. It means they are worth more than the offense. Amen.

Be kind to one another,

tender-hearted, forgiving

each other.

Ephesians 4:32

Mutterings

In matters of forgiveness
there is always a
prisoner—the one needing
forgiveness or the one
withholding forgiveness.

—Anonymous

Green Mountain

Canine Retreat

Something to ◆ Chew on

There are places where troubled hearts find solace in the company of good friends and their Creator. Visit them as often as you can.

They are known by many names: Shangri-La … The Secret Garden … Eden. Some reside only in the imagination, but others are quite real. They are places where the silence can whisper truth to the deep regions of the heart. In my youth, such a place was Green Mountain.

Green is one of three mountains ringing Boulder, Colorado. George and I hiked that mountain whenever the need surfaced to sort things out.

Our destination was a brass plate marking the top of Green Mountain. Sitting up there with George in my lap, I could survey most of South Boulder and the things that troubled me. A broken heart took me to that place at least three times. The reality that I was headed for Vietnam if my grades didn't improve drove me there one spring day. But most of my trips were prompted by a vague confusion over what to do with my life.

You can talk things out with a dog and never wonder if he is judging you or will reject you for mouthing dark thoughts. Some dogs sense when you're troubled and offer the comfort of a warm muzzle. George always pressed his body against me, a tangible

80

◆ ◆ ◆ ◆ ◆ ◆ ◆ ◆ ◆ ◆ ◆ ◆ ◆ ◆

touch to anchor my mental wanderings.

Through the years, life came more into focus. I graduated from college and then grad school. I learned that I was free to fail, not free not to try, and that I was more free than I thought. George and I still sought out Green Mountain when I was home. His gait was a bit slower. But he still offered me the wondrous gift of an ear in which I could pour out all my longings and doubts.

There were no blinding revelations for me on that mountain. But I did find solace in the company of that little dog, a mountaintop, and the Creator of it all.

In his later years, George couldn't make the round trip on his own. He'd gamely set the pace across the ridge, but the trip back found his old bones too tired. Eventually, he'd give up and sit down, and then I knew he was ready to accept a ride wrapped around my shoulders.

I haven't been back to Green Mountain in a long time.

Civilization now blocks my old route to the top and that brass-plated boulder. I still have plenty to sort out: a family, a job, and a calling. My wife, Luci, and I have found other places to listen to whispered truths, but she offers me far more than an ear. She offers an understanding heart.

Green Mountain will likely be there until the end of time. But George is long gone, and with

him, much of the enchantment of that place. The ideas and values that circulated around Boulder back in the sixties have spawned a host of competing truths. I am less troubled by them now. Certain of far less, I am confident of "the better part" granted by the One who keeps track of the sparrows, the hairs on my head, and old hiking companions who once pressed close.

Paws **for** Prayer

Father, thank you for meeting me in ways I can understand and for never, ever missing one of our appointed times together. Amen.

And I will keep watch to see

what He will speak to me.

Habakkuk 2:1

Mutterings

Our sense of God's
presence is often in inverse
proportion to the pace of
our lives.

—Richard Swenson

Truffle

No Easy Way Out

Something to ♥ Chew on

When you're really stuck, tennis-ball solutions aren't worth much. You may need a member of the family to put in a good word for you.

If ever a dog was misnamed, it was Truffle. Truffle is a sweet, French, feminine sort of name. A dog named Truffle ought to be petite, pink, and Pekinese. Nothing could be further from the truth. Truffle weighed around 120 pounds. Truffle was a he— black as midnight and fiercely protective.

The first time I met Truffle was the day before my roommate and I were to house-and-hound sit for an acquaintance in Los Angeles. The mistress of the house introduced me to Truffle after assuring Truffle that I was harmless and probably wouldn't taste all that good.

Eventually, Truffle "permitted" me to throw his tennis ball so that he could fetch it. The rest of Truffle's human family assured me that I had now passed muster and would be instantly welcomed upon my next visit. Still, they suggested that it might be prudent to take one of Truffle's balls along with me just to remind him that we were now friends.

The next evening, I entered Truffle's house through the kitchen, tennis ball in hand. From the bowels of the house, I heard the deep-throated wail of one thirsting for human blood. The floors

84

♡ ♥ ♡ ♡ ♥ ♡ ♡ ♥ ♡ ♡ ♥ ♡ ♡ ♥ ♡

shook as I felt Truffle thundering in my direction. I stopped with my shoulder braced against the swinging door that separated the kitchen from the rest of the house.

"Hello, Truffle. Nice Truffle."

Truffle's momentum forced open the door enough for me to see his snarling, fang-infested snout. Fortunately, he wasn't able to get through. I managed to hold the edge of the swinging door as high up as I could reach, and Truffle continued his imitation of a battering ram. I reviewed my options.

There was no way to lock the swinging door separating me from Truffle. The doorway through which I had entered was fifteen feet away—much too far to make a run for it. The house was isolated, so there was no point in calling for help.

Miraculously, I was still holding Truffle's tennis ball. "Nice Truffle. Good Truffle." I allowed the door to open enough to push the ball into Truffle's side. Through the crack, I watched Truffle snag the ball with lightning reflexes and then snap it in two with his powerful jaws. Not a promising sign.

An hour later, I was still holding the door against Truffle when I heard a car in the driveway. My roommate, along with a member of the family who had decided to check on my progress, had arrived!

Truffle eventually forgave me my trespasses and agreed to

♥ ♥ ♥ ♥ ♥ ♥ ♥ ♥ ♥ ♥ ♥ ♥ ♥ ♥ ♥

let me live. During the week that followed, we became good friends. I wouldn't want to say he mellowed all that much under my tutelage, however. During the week we house sat, Truffle managed to bite a security guard who wandered into the backyard unannounced. Pour soul, I bet he didn't even have a tennis ball.

Paws **for** Prayer

Father God, you never leave me to fend for myself. May my heart catch up with my head and feel the certainty of that truth. Amen.

He is able also to save

forever those who draw

near to God through Him.

Hebrews 7:25

Mutterings

Oh, to be vouched for!
Now, oh, there's the ticket!

—Anonymous

The Eighteen-Month Dog

The Loaner Puppy

Once I'd assured my wife that having a dog didn't mean that our house would smell like a kennel, we signed up with Guide Dogs of the Desert to socialize one of their puppies. We thought we were headed overseas as soon as I finished my doctorate, and this was the only way we could realistically have a pet in the interim. The downside would be having to give him up after eighteen months of training for his future mission.

"Be careful," we were told. "Don't get attached. He won't really be yours."

A month later, we picked up our Labrador puppy. He came with a name already attached—Griffin.

Griffin looked like a little pig with way too much skin. He grunted, frowned, and strained when you picked him up, and had puppy smell all over him. Luci was a goner at first sight. Griffin also came with a set of instructions, a green vest with GUIDE DOGS OF THE DESERT PUPPY stenciled across the back, and an official-looking card that allowed Griffin to go where other pets were not allowed to tread.

The first time I tried to walk him through the automatic doors of a department store, you'd have thought he was ascending the steps to a guillotine. Elevators must have seemed like boarding a rocket ship to the moon. When I presented him with a newly polished linoleum floor, he hunkered down like a raw recruit crawling under a barbed-wire obstacle course with live ammunition flying overhead.

Within a few weeks, he'd mastered most of the challenges and welcomed this brave new world. We were successful trainers of a soon-to-be guide dog!

Guard your heart. Remember, he's only on loan.

The roly-poly puppy, who used to squeeze between the bars of our wrought-iron fence, grew into a long-limbed Labrador with a classic wisdom knot on the top of his head. A backyard seldom visited became an oasis of life and laughter and neighborhood kids.

Griffin's eighteen-month stay passed quickly. We threw a going-away party, and about thirty of our neighbors came. We laughed and lingered over our good-byes. We took dozens of photo keepsakes of something we couldn't keep.

"How can you bear to let him go?"

I don't know.

The trainers at Guide Dogs of the Desert were practiced veterans in the rituals of letting go. They gave us space and time for our private good-byes. They welcomed us behind the scenes and explained the months of special training through which each future guide dog would go. They enfolded us into the

● ● ● ● ● ● ● ● ● ● ● ● ● ●

noble cause for which we'd signed on eighteen months earlier. They promised to keep us informed of Griffin's progress and ultimate placement.

"Give it a few months and see if you'd be willing to take another puppy-in-training for us."

We shut the car door on the sound of twenty Golden Labradors barking and playing in the background and began the long drive home. We'd barely left the driveway before the tears came.

I didn't know this could hurt so much. I didn't think we could do this sort of thing again.

During the next three weeks, I repaired the backyard. No more holes. No more chewed shoes. Less hassles. But fewer moments. Then the phone rang.

"Griffin is a great dog, but he isn't going to be a guide dog. He has severe hip dysplasia. He will likely only live another eighteen months before the problem would force you to put him down. Would you be willing to take him back?"

"… I don't know."

For momentary, light affliction is producing for us an eternal weight of glory far beyond all comparison.

2 Corinthians 4:17

Paws for Prayer

Dear God, remind me once again that your will never leads me where your grace won't sustain me. Amen.

Mutterings

I can look back at my darkest periods and realize that these were the times when the Lord was holding me closest. But I couldn't see his face because my face was in his breast—crying.

—John Michael Talbot

The Agreement

A Contract of Love

When Guide Dogs of the Desert offered to give Griffin back to us, I wasn't sure. It was so painful to give Griff up the first time. It broke Luci's heart. Griff was her first dog. My heart was in worse shape than hers.

I could picture the future. Eventually, Griffin's hind legs would give out, and he'd be reduced to dragging himself around. One day, we'd have to put him down. No matter how I played out the story, it had a sad ending.

Luci was of a different mind. "I don't know what the future holds for Griffin, but I want us to share it with him. We can love him through it all. We're the only family he's ever known."

"Sweetheart, do you understand what we'd be letting ourselves in for? I'm afraid the pain of watching him suffer will tear our hearts more than letting him go the first time."

"You may be right, but I don't want to miss the love we can have just because we're afraid of the pain to come."

She was right.

We cried some and wrote out an agreement to which we would hold when faced with the painful decisions that would inevitably follow:

A Contract of Love

■ ■ ■ ■ ■ ■ ■ ■ ■ ■ ■ ■ ■ ■ ■ ■ ■

First, we place this little dog back into his Creator's care. We acknowledge that he is only on loan for a short time. We're trusting that the lessons learned will offset the pain involved.

Second, we will not take heroic steps to prolong Griffin's life. There will be no major surgery—only love and care.

Third, we will not allow the future pain to rob us of the present joys or shadow the memories of a boon companion. We resolve to risk our hearts again to God's creatures after this one is gone.

I wrote that contract more than ten years ago. We haven't needed it. I guess Griffin's bones calcified enough to spare him from the earlier prognosis. He has enjoyed a fairly pain-free life. Luci was right. The inevitability of future pain hasn't robbed us of a decade of loving Griffin. We also didn't miss the stories and lessons of the heart that follow.

Paws for Prayer

Father God, it's hard in my myopic state to look beyond the pain of the moment. Fix my eyes on you, the focal point of saving faith. Amen.

Consider it all joy, my brethren, when you encounter various trials, knowing that the testing of your faith produces endurance.

James 1:2–3

Mutterings

Enjoy when you can and
endure when you must.

—Johann Wolfgang von
Goethe

It's a Mouth Thing

He'll Eat Anything ... Almost

Something to ◆ Chew on

A lack of discernment always leaves a bad taste in someone's mouth.

It is a well-known fact that two-year-olds and puppy dogs will put just about anything into their mouths. And what's mulled over in the mouth usually leaves an indelible mark upon the chewer or the chewed.

A friend of mine once took his two-year-old boy to the circus. It seems the high point of the outing was the cotton candy. Take a cup of raw sugar, zap it with a whirling electro convergence thingamabob and presto! You have cotton candy—99 percent air and 99 percent sugar. (How do you suppose that's possible?)

A couple of days later, the same two-year-old cotton-candy junkie spied a large spider's web in the corner of the garage, complete with flies. This child was not unsupervised. Dad watched the whole thing. "A learning experience," he called it. I never thought about the obvious similarities between a spider's web and cotton candy, but it was easy to see where the story was headed. A tiny hand gathered in the deserted web, dead flies and all, and proceeded to make the disgusting discovery that all that's white, airy, and cottony isn't sweet.

Griffin made discoveries similar to that two-year-old as he

chewed through his puppyhood. Among his list of chewables were the left mate of my favorite pair of shoes, the nose of an expensive stuffed animal I bought Luci before we were married, the leg of our oak coffee table, the phone receiver, the garden hose with a lifetime guarantee against "normal wear," various cooking utensils, every plant in the backyard, and assorted toys belonging to visiting children to which the children had bonded for life and would never be able to accept the loss even when I offered to buy them a new and improved one.

Griffin no longer feels compelled to chew everything in sight, but give him a grape, a slice of apple, or any "marginal" goody, and he'll mull it around in his mouth for a while, spit it out on the carpet, and push it with his nose. Once it has a sufficient amount of carpet fuzz stuck on it, he'll eat it.

He'll Eat Anything ... Almost

◆ ◆ ◆ ◆ ◆ ◆ ◆ ◆ ◆ ◆ ◆ ◆ ◆ ◆ ◆

I still remember the day Griffin finally caught his first fly. I guess you could call it a learning experience. I didn't know he could make such a face or wipe his tongue on our carpet at a dead run.

Paws **for** Prayer

O Father, help me to develop a greater appetite for you. Amen.

How sweet are Your words

to my taste!

Psalm 119:103

Mutterings

Choose rather to punish
your appetites than be
punished by them.

—Tyrius Maximus

Drool Is Just a Fact of Life

The Animal Cracker Drama

When the neighborhood kids are two years of age, they can stand eye to eye and nose to nose with Griff. Over the years, certain boundaries have been established for such encounters. First, it is acknowledged by one and all that Griffin is in no way responsible for what his tail does. Whether it's sending some kid flying or clearing all the Christmas-tree ornaments on the lower branches, Griffin remains blissfully ignorant of his tail's transgressions and thus without culpability. However, transgressions occurring at Griffin's other end are not tolerated. Mugging small children to gain their cracker, candy, or any other munchie simply isn't allowed.

Bethany, a petite two-year-old blonde full of curls, was a tentative eater at best. Her parents had house-and-hound sat for us on several occasions. Bethany and Griffin were both well aware of the twin boundaries that governed their relationship. She'd nibble around the edges of her animal cracker and then set it in front of her on our deck.

Griffin took all this in from the closest possible distance (a bit

Something to ♥ Chew on

Delayed gratification doesn't mean no gratification. It's the promise of better later.

100

less than an inch). The suitcase that doubles as Griffin's nose quivered longingly, inhaling the aroma that lingers on all animal crackers. Like one of those red-billed, bulb-tailed toy birds that continually dips its beak into a glass of water, Griffin followed the journey of the cracker from Bethany's mouth to the deck and back again. Bethany was oblivious to the internal struggle of her companion.

As I chanced upon this little drama, it was obvious that both players had been there for quite a while. Griffin's front was soaked, and he was sitting in a sizable puddle of drool that inched ever closer to the nibbled cracker. There are some things that you can't control in life, and outward obedience usually comes with an inward price.

Bethany finally abandoned her half-eaten cracker at the edge of the puddle, and Griffin remained frozen in a classic approach-avoidance mode, caught in his own internal conflict. It was a moment of great pride for me—a trustworthy companion whose training proved sound. I took mercy on him and said the release word, "Okay." The cracker vanished.

Paws **for** Prayer

O Father, help me to enjoy the fruits of freedom without falling off the narrow suspension bridge of discipline. Amen.

All discipline for the moment

seems not to be joyful …

yet to those who have been

trained by it … it yields the

peaceful fruit of

righteousness.

Hebrews 12:11

Mutterings

The first and best victory
is to conquer self.

—Plato

The Nose

Better Than a Handshake

Griffin has a magnificent nose. Over the years, it has been a colorful billboard of his maturation. The puppy pink of his nostrils gave way to adult black, and now it has the splotched appearance of old age. His downy white muzzle turned soft golden during his first eighteen months, and now it is silky gray.

I've always been a "nose man." The nose is the lighthouse to one's character—a beacon of things to come—right out there in front of everything else, taking the lead and pointing the way. That's where God put them, and that's where noses belong.

Griffin's nose is as intricate as it is large—a cavernous monument to olfactory excellence! There are two little muscles just behind each nostril that quiver and pulse in the presence of any interesting aroma. The sides of his nostrils end in commalike curves. Griffin can curl the entire rim of each nostril under, much the way an elephant can tuck the end of its trunk around a peanut—the miracle of ingenuity.

Griffin has suffered the indignity of having numerous objects placed on the top part of his nose after being told to "Stay!" He

Something to ● Chew on

Look and listen, taste and touch, and don't forget to smell. Some of the best memories are accessed only through the nose.

can balance a tennis ball, then roll his head sideways and catch the ball in his mouth. His record for holding a biscuit on his nose is just under six minutes.

The nose never sleeps. Just try placing a doggy treat in front of a snoozing Griffin. It won't be long before the smell sensors that take up approximately 99 percent of his brain have raffled the rest of the dog into action. *Crunch. Crunch. Crunch.*

Griffin's nose is much more than a nose. It is a handshake at the front door after a hard day. It is the tip of an iceberg, wedging itself between Luci and me to share in the warmth of a hug. It is a substitute doorbell, rattling the sliding-glass door to be let in. And on those late-night vigils when the desktop computer defies my efforts to write, Griffin's nose finds its way into my lap and reminds me that life is worth celebrating, whether I write another word or not.

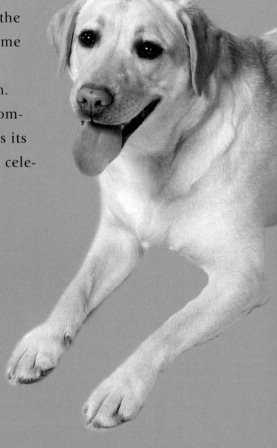

● ● ● ● ● ● ● ● ● ● ● ● ● ● ●

Paws **for** Prayer

Loving Creator, you are never more present than when I bury my face into the garments of your embrace and inhale. Amen.

I will give thanks to You,

for I am fearfully and

wonderfully made.

Psalm 139:14

Mutterings

A nose by any other name
would smell the same.

The Designated Digging Area

If You Can't Beat 'Em, Join 'Em

When Griffin was a pup, chewing was at the top of his list of favorite activities. But his adolescence was given over to digging. Griffin began a trench between two of our palm trees. Why he felt the need for a trench was beyond me. It didn't really go anywhere. I lectured, scolded, and cajoled all to no effect. I filled in, resodded, and roped off the wounded areas.

You may be able to separate the dog from his digging, but you can't take the digging out of the dog. Eventually, I spread chicken wire over the repaired areas and let the grass grow up through it. Clever but not very smart. Griffin adapted to the new restrictions by digging a trench between two other palm trees, as well as a few random holes on the side of the house.

Short of covering the entire yard with chicken wire, there would always be a hole in our backyard. Griffin was a dedicated digger.

Years earlier, I tried to change my best friend into a punctual person. Mike was one of the most loving, caring, fun-to-be-around people you could ever hope to meet. However, he was always thirty minutes late. You could make him write it down, stress how important it was to be on time. Lecture. Scold. Cajole. Nothing worked.

Something to ■ Chew on

Don't be too quick to take the dig out of the dog, or you may end up with a bigger hole than you started with.

108

If You Can't Beat 'Em, Join 'Em

■ ■ ■ ■ ■ ■ ■ ■ ■ ■ ■ ■ ■ ■ ■ ■ ■

I experimented with telling him that whatever we were doing was happening thirty minutes earlier than actually planned. I lied. I soon figured it wasn't a particularly good trade-off—punctuality at the cost of the truth. Finally, as an act of sheer willpower, Mike agreed to be on time "no matter what." Well, on time he was. Caring, fun-loving, and delightful to be around, he wasn't.

Within a week, all of his friends were begging him to go back to being late. We missed the old Mike. Luci finally came to Griff's and my rescue with a solution of her own. "If you can't stop Griffin from digging, why not encourage him to focus his attention on just one place—a designated digging area?" I surveyed all of his holes and picked out his favorite spot at the base of a palm tree. Then I built a box around it and encouraged Griff to dig to his heart's content. Dig he did. On more than one occasion, I thought he'd escaped the back-yard, only to later find him asleep hidden in the depths of his designated digging area.

That spot ceased to be an eyesore and instead became a special part of the yard. Everyone wondered why there was a boxed-in hole near the palm tree. Griffin's sand box? A concession to genetics? A necessary evil? Not a chance. The designated digging area is a visual celebration of who Griffin is—a wonderful Labrador who digs people and holes.

Paws **for** Prayer

Father, may I be less bothered about the imperfections in others and more concerned about my own transformation. Amen.

And do not be conformed to

this world, but be

transformed by the

renewing of your mind.

Romans 12:2

Mutterings

We only listen to
those instincts which are
our own.

—Jean de La Fontaine

Griffin and the Jacuzzi

Easy Come, Easy Go

After Griffin made fifty dollars for his ever-so-brief portrayal of Old Yeller in a Disney promo, Luci and I started to joke about getting a Jacuzzi when Griffin earned enough to buy one. I could almost feel the pulsating waters swirling around my aching muscles as I lowered myself into the steamy spa waters! But then Griffin's acting career "dried up" so to speak. Good-bye, Jacuzzi.

A year later, Luci and I were headed to Jelgava, Latvia, for a six-month teaching stint at the Agricultural University when our friends who cast Griffin in his Old Yeller cameos gave us a call.

"Disney's doing a remake of *The Incredible Journey*. We think Griffin would be good as one of the leads. Shooting could take up to six months. Would you be willing to let us keep him for that long?"

"Give up our dog for six months? That's a long time."

"Well, give it some thought and let us know."

"When would the movie be made?"

"We're scheduled to begin this fall."

The exact time Luci and I would be in Jelgava!

Hello, Jacuzzi!

If you've seen the movie *Homeward Bound,* you know that the older

Easy Come, Easy Go

dog, Shadow, is a Golden Retriever and not a Golden Labrador. It took them two weeks to decide between Griffin and the other dog named Ben. Ben, with the voice of Don Ameche, went on to stardom as Shadow. Griffin went home. Good-bye, Jacuzzi.

I've often wondered how things might have turned out had Griffin been cast in that movie instead of Ben. Would our lives have changed in any significant way? Hollywood premieres. Celebrity appearances. Radio interviews with Griffin's family. Jacuzziing every night!

Griffin never gave any of it a second thought. Luci and I have always been audience enough for him.

A few years later, some dear friends were moving into a new house and asked if we'd like their old spa. Hello, Jacuzzi!

Luci and I have enjoyed that old spa as much as we thought we would. It's a great way to end the day. We have time to talk and reflect as we soak. Still, I've never been able to coax Griffin to join us. I suppose it looks too much like a bath to him.

We're moving to New York soon, a long way from southern California. It's too far to take an old Jacuzzi. I'll miss it. Griffin won't. Good-bye, Jacuzzi.

I can't help but wonder if Griffin may yet get us another Jacuzzi. After all, he's the inspiration behind these stories.

Easy Come, Easy Go

◆ ◆ ◆ ◆ ◆ ◆ ◆ ◆ ◆ ◆ ◆ ◆ ◆ ◆ ◆

Paws **for** Prayer

*Faithful God, thank you for your earthly as
well as transcendent pleasures. Amen.*

Furthermore, as for every

man to whom God has

given riches and wealth, He

has also empowered him to

eat from them and to

receive his reward.

Ecclesiastes 5:19

Mutterings

A man is rich in
proportion to the number
of things he can afford to
let alone.

—Henry David Thoreau

A Short Course in the Ways of Hide-and-Seek

Part One: Hiding to Be Found

Griffin's Rules

Something to ♥ Chew on

Keep looking, and you'll discover that life is less about winning and losing and more about finding and being found.

Suppressed giggles. Heart pounding. Living on the edge of discovery. Stay put or make a break for it. What other game has so much to offer? And that's only the "hiding" half of it! The thrills of hide-and-seek never grow stale. Unless, of course, they stop seeking and don't bother to tell you. Griffin would never do that.

Hide in a closet, behind a chair, or under the bed. Give a quick whistle, and you soon hear the sounds of Griffin's search. The game is on!

With Griff, it might be better to call it a game of hide-n-sniff. Griff looks with his nose. Oh, he occasionally barks at the wrong closed door. My scent is all over the house. But it isn't long before he restarts his search. Griff will retrace his steps a hundred times. I've never seen him quit. He looks until he finds.

Once I hid too well—scrunched down, in the dark, behind a pile of dirty clothes in the corner of the closet. A pair of ripe tennis shoes masked my scent. Griff searched and searched, round and round. He looked. I hid. We both grew weary. It took too long.

116

I developed a cramp in my right leg. Wedged under the hanger rod, a knot developed in my left shoulder.

Then I started thinking, *What are you trying to prove? That you are the master of hide-and-seek in this house? Has anyone challenged your exalted position as the Viscount of Vanishing? Does Griffin even play to win? I always play to win. Why bother if you aren't trying to win?*

Come to think of it, Luci isn't all that interested in winning either. She hates to see anyone lose. Games are a vehicle for interpersonal interaction with her, not an exercise in domination. She'd rather everybody won.

I think I've been in this closet too long.

When I finally came out of hiding, Griffin's response was the same as if he'd found me. No sense of defeat here. No chagrined you-really-got-me-this-time look. Griff and I weren't playing by the same rules. Every one of our games of hide-and-seek ends with a tail-wagging, ear-rubbing celebration. There's just something about finding and being found that Griffin thinks calls for a party.

I think I like Griffin's rules better than the ones I've been playing by:

> *Passion: seeking after.*
> *Longing: to be sought after.*
> *Celebration: of being back together happily*
> *ever after.*

Griffin's Rules

Paws for Prayer

Father God, thank you for making your presence so obvious. I would never have found you on my own. Amen.

I permitted Myself to

be found by those who

did not seek Me. I said,

"Here am I, here am I."

Isaiah 65:1

Mutterings

Watch your thoughts; they become words. Watch your words; they become actions. Watch your actions; they become habits. Watch your habits; they become character. Watch your character; it becomes your destiny.

—Frank Outlaw

Part Two: Hiding Not to Be Found

Gary's Rules

Something to ● Chew on

Don't hide from help or flee from friends.

Little kids love to hide in order to be found. Not so with dogs. Dogs hide *not* to be found. Run some water in the bath tub, and bring in a few extra towels, a plastic pitcher, and some dog shampoo. ZOOM! Griff goes into hiding every time. How does he know?

Call. Cajole. Command. It's pretty much a waste of time. He won't come. You have to go and find him. Usually, he's hiding under the dining-room table, in the far corner of the living room, or behind Luci.

Reluctant to the bone, Gruff delays, retreats, rolls on his back with paws tight to the chest. He's a blob of defeat, seeking mercy from a prone, penitent position. Poor, pathetic thing!

"What's the big deal? It's only a bath! And you really need one."

The thing is, when it's all over, Griffin is in his most celebratory mood. Toweled down, shaken off, free to roam, he runs through the house. And from somewhere deep inside, he resonates the most contented sound known in dogdom, "GGRRAAAUGHH!"

Griffin isn't the only one who hides so he won't be found. I'm prone to do some hiding of my own come bath time. When life gets messy and I'm losing control, it's hard not to hide.

We both like life to run in comfortable and predictable patterns. We both tolerate a considerable amount of personal messiness without feeling the need to be cleaned. We both like to sort things out on our own with little outside interference. Griffin has little talent for hiding. I wish I could say the same for me.

I have many layers I can hide behind—masks of my own making. Just ask Luci. She'll tell you that masquerades often aren't the "ball" they're touted to be. She hates masks—mine and hers.

Somehow I get the notion that the real me isn't good enough. It isn't safe to come out of hiding. I doubt the motives of anyone who comes looking for me with anything looking like a washrag.

It has been that way from the very beginning. The first question asked of the first man was, "Where are you?" Adam, hiding not to be found, was found out. The best thing that could have happened to him after his forbidden snack was for God to say, "Bath time, Adam! You really need one. Stop slinking around. Once you're clean, you'll feel like dancing. I promise."

Gary's Rules

●●●●●●●●●●●●●●●●

In the notable poem by Francis Thompson, "The Hound of Heaven" chases us down the corridors of time, sniffs us out, dogs our days, and we flee from God in terror. We hide in darkness. Then one day, with nowhere to turn, no mask within reach, we face our lifelong hunter. The Hound of Heaven approaches, not to devour our souls, but to wash our feet and make us clean.

Paws **for Prayer**

Father God, I have an ostrich faith that sticks its head in the ground and thinks safe. I give you permission to pull a few tailfeathers whenever I go into hiding.
Amen.

Wash me, and I shall be

whiter than snow.

Psalm 51:7

Mutterings

My will and God's sovereignty meet at the point of obedience.

—Jeannette Cliff George

Part Three: Hiding to Be Missed

God's Rules

Without a doubt, the biggest problem I've had with Griffin is getting him to come when I call. I could give him much more freedom if he responded immediately. I could trust him not to chase a cat across the street or sniff the wrong dog, if only he came the instant I called. He doesn't.

In the house, his obedience is near perfection. But, put him in the park across the street, and obedience is played out on his terms. Every tree and bush requires his closest attention. Why, how could he even entertain the possibility of responding to my call when such important matters lie between us?

Delayed obedience is still disobedience, and his disobedience results in a loss of freedom. Who wants to come home under those terms?

Griffin isn't the only one who drags his feet when he should come running. The problem is that Griffin and I have our own ideas about appropriate response time. We see little connection between tomorrow's freedom and our actions in the park today.

I have discovered a remedy to Griffin's delayed obedience syndrome. It's called hiding to be missed. If I step behind a tree

Something to ▪ Chew on

You can't enjoy a romp in the park for long if you've lost track of the One who brought you there in the first place.

124

while Griff is on his sniff-and-lift mission, he soon realizes I'm gone. As long as he can keep track of me, he feels in control, but being on his own is another matter. Head erect, he scans the park. Still as stone, he listens. Forget the bushes that need marking. More important business is at hand. "My master is missing. I may be all alone in the park. Not good. I better find Gary right now!"

When Griffin finally spots me, he comes running. His tail wags. All concern vanishes. Once more everything is right with the world. Bonds far stronger than a leash are reestablished.

It seems to me that God does some hiding of his own. He steps into the background. He is not where we left him. He, too, hides to be missed.

Ever noticed the hiding-to-be-missed verses in the Bible? *"Seek and you will find." "Search for Me with all your heart." "It is the glory of God to conceal a thing."* Who can truly enjoy a romp in the park when God's whereabouts aren't known?

In the ways of hide-and-seek, there's always a tension between the one searching and the one being sought, a delicate balance between being taken for granted and taking too long.

Paws **for** Prayer

Dear Father, if you didn't deliberately stay in the background, every knee would bow under the power of your presence. But the ability to choose would cease to exist, and I wouldn't be able to freely miss you and seek after you. Amen.

He is not far from each

one of us.

Acts 17:27

Mutterings

Oneness only comes at the price of independence.

—Dan Jarrell

Dog Bite

Eating My Own Words

Ever been bitten by a dog? I have.

At first the shock of it masks the pain. Then rapid-fire questions crisscross the synapses of your brain. *Did he break the skin? Was he foaming at the mouth? Why didn't you get a name and phone number?*

Five minutes later, there's a more defined pain. You check for damage. Coat sleeve torn. A deep bluish-red pucker marks your forearm. Not much blood yet. You squeeze it to make it bleed, to wash out the wound. It doesn't work.

An hour later, you feel sick to your stomach. *Have to lie down. Weak. This is silly. It was only one tooth. Ironic. Poetic justice. Wait till the others hear.*

The Iron Curtain had yet to fall, and I was doing an evangelism seminar in Riga, Latvia. A dozen hardy souls had gathered for training. The police state had softened its stance. Sharing one's convictions in a public place was now possible. What once could land you in prison was now tolerated. Freedom of speech was fast becoming a reality. *Glasnost* had become a household word.

"We're going to have a great time this afternoon," I told the group. "I suspect most of us are a bit hesitant. But all we are

You usually have to swallow your words when you bite off more than you can chew.

128

♦ ♦ ♦ ♦ ♦ ♦ ♦ ♦ ♦ ♦ ♦ ♦ ♦ ♦

going to do is talk to people and listen to what they have to say. Don't worry, the folks we're going to talk to won't bite."

After completing the training, we were ready to put it into practice. We divided into groups of two and headed for the park, the Freedom Monument, and Old Town.

In those days, English speakers were hard to find. So I had to settle for my own efforts at pantomime and a Latvian tract. A well-dressed woman with a Rottweiler at her side crossed the park in my direction. I smiled and said, "Rottweiler," pointing at her dog. She smiled and nodded, our two languages apparently sharing this particular word.

Surprised to find an American in her country, she stopped. I showed her my tract, and she patiently read while I held the booklet. I'd just turned the page when her four-legged companion lunged and bit me. She quickly pulled him back on a short leash. The dog seemed to think that he'd made his point and showed no signs of renewing his attack. Perhaps he had resented the intrusion to his daily walk. Unexpectedly, he bit me just at the precise moment the booklet addressed the depraved nature of humanity. Maybe he resented the idea or was just embellishing the point.

I got a blend of snickers and sympathy when we

◆ ◆ ◆ ◆ ◆ ◆ ◆ ◆ ◆ ◆ ◆ ◆ ◆ ◆ ◆

gathered to debrief at the end of the afternoon. The others delighted in reminding me of my assurances that no one was going to get bitten. The teacher always learns more than the student. I still carry the scar on my right forearm as a reminder.

Paws **for** Prayer

Pierced Lord, perhaps those who suffer little for their faith have little faith to suffer for. It is almost too scary to say what must come next. Enlarge the horizons of my faith.
Amen.

Indeed, all who desire to live

godly in Christ Jesus will be

persecuted.

2 Timothy 3:12

Mutterings

If I ever wonder about the appropriate "spiritual" response to pain and suffering, I can note how Jesus responded to his own: with fear and trembling, with loud cries and tears.

—Philip Yancey

Deception Clues

Helicopter Ears

Communication experts have long studied the unconscious ways we signal our hidden guilt and deception. It is called "leakage."

If you fidget with your hands, mumble, shift your feet, and fail to make eye contact, odds are you're "leaking." Some of us are good at deception. Some of us are pathetic. I've never met a dog who was any good at deception. Too many things give them away.

With Waddles, it was her tail. The way she tucked it under her bottom as a pup was a sure sign of guilt. It was time to check the house for puddles.

George couldn't make eye contact if he thought he was guilty of something. I remember wondering one day just how many chocolate chip cookies George could consume. After he trotted off with his tenth cookie, I became suspicious. Same smile, same wag, but he couldn't look me in the face. "George? What are you up to?" It turned out he was stashing them all over the house—under furniture, in the closet, behind the bookshelf. I couldn't begin to find all of them, but the ants sure did.

Griffin's main source of deception leakage is his ears. Griff has a way of holding his ears so that the bottom halves bend straight out. Luci and I call them his "helicopter ears." One evening, he wandered into the living room acting a bit strange. I noticed a single piece of orange twine barely sticking out of his mouth.

"Griffin? Come here. Let me see what you've got in your mouth." Helicopter ears! Ah ha! Got ya! The ever-compliant Griffin dutifully sat in front of me, jaws clenched, ears bent in the middle. I pried open his mouth only to discover that he was holding an entire stuffed toy lion in his mouth! The telltale bit of string was part of the lion's orange tail.

The things we try to keep secret! It turns out deception leakage is a good thing. All of us need to get caught once in a while. A stuffed toy lion isn't much of a problem unless you end up swallowing it. I know. I've swallowed more than my share of harmful things.

Helicopter Ears

Paws for Prayer

Father, you read me like an open book. Please dog-ear the pages of my life that I need to revisit so that I may ask for forgiveness. Amen.

The one who desires life, to

love and see good days,

must keep his tongue from

evil and his lips from

speaking deceit.

1 Peter 3:10

Mutterings

You can fool all the people
some of the time, and some of
the people all the time, but you
can't fool Mom.

—Anonymous

Second Fiddle to a Dog Biscuit

Stopping at the Tollbooth

There's a natural affection built into Labradors. If Luci and I are in different rooms, Griff will position himself in the hallway so he can keep track of his family. Sit still for long, and Griff's economy-size nose will find its way under your hand.

Still, there is one moment when Griff wants nothing to do with affection. Walk by his "tollbooth" (the pantry where his dog biscuits are kept), and all thoughts of affection take a backseat to what's inside the pantry door. A creature of habit, he heads for his tollbooth whenever he's been outside. Griff takes up his station on the edge of the carpet, ears erect, head tilted, still as death. He's just so darn fetching! All you want to do is give him a big hug and scratch behind his ear. Dream on!

Trying to pet Griffin in front of the pantry is like trying to put a super-charged worm on a fishhook. Can't be done. Waste of time. Don't even try. Rubs him the wrong way when affection delays his divine right to a goody.

It happened again early this morning when Griffin whined me out of bed. I marched down the hall across the cold kitchen floor, pulled open the sliding-glass door, and welcomed the Griffmeister

Something to ● Chew on

If you have too many tollbooths in your life you'll never get where the love is.

back from the wilds of the backyard. Straight to his tollbooth. Ears erect. Head tilted. He looked so doggone huggable. I walked over and extended a loving hand. You'd have thought I had a cattle prod and some nasty intentions. He ducked my hand and resisted my affectionate overtures. He lets me know in no uncertain terms that our agendas are light years apart.

Oh, well. The demanded treat is placed into Griff's mouth. The nonrelational ritual is over. Expectation met. Rebuff accepted. I hear sounds of crunching as I walk down the hall to the bedroom.

A few minutes later, I hear the unmistakable sound of paws clipping the carpet as Griff makes his way into our bedroom. Feigning sleep, I soon feel the familiar touch of Griffin's muzzle under my hand. Companionship is now restored on his terms. It's hard to play second fiddle to a dog biscuit.

God knows just how I feel. I do the same thing to him all the time. I'm more interested in his hand than his heart.

"I know. I know. But just let me read the newspaper first, then we'll spend some time together. Don't press so close. I've got work to do, deadlines to meet, and I need some inspiration for the next chapter. After that, I'll clip along and let you love on me. But not now. What

I'd really like is for you to open your hand, not your heart. See how straight I sit, countenance focused, visibly worthy. Give me what I want first, and then I'll accept the offer of yourself."

My stomach keeps crowding in front of my soul. Feeding the flesh becomes more important than savoring the fellowship. Some days I'm no smarter than my dog.

Paws **for** Prayer

Father God, only you can satisfy my deepest hunger. Please curb my appetite for lesser things. Amen.

Do not worry then, saying, "What will we eat?" … But seek first His kingdom and His righteousness, and all these things will be added to you.

Matthew 6:31, 33

Mutterings

Satan will give you
everything you want. God
will give you everything
you need.

—Anonymous

A Front-Yard Life

A Dog for Backyard People

We used to live on a cul-de-sac with twelve houses, about twenty kids, a few cats, and eight or nine dogs. Since we lived on the corner, the side of our backyard faced the street, making Griffin more of a front-yard dog.

When Griffin was younger, he put his chew toys on the other side of the fence to encourage a bit of play from the kids on their way home from school. As he grew older, he snoozed near that same sidewalk, ready with a friendly wag for all who passed his way.

The other dogs on our street were backyard dogs, hidden behind wooden or wrought-iron gates set well back from the street. Three of the dogs visited Griffin on their daily walks to the park across the street. A few of the neighborhood dogs, I only saw once or twice. The existence of one dog, I could confirm solely on the basis of its bark.

It's hard to get to know a backyard dog. It's not any easier to get to know backyard people.

Today, it seems we prefer to drive into the garage, close the automatic door, and go about our business. Cocooned. Insulated.

Something to ■ Chew on

If you keep to your own backyard, there will be little opportunity to celebrate and be celebrated.

140

Ignorant of the neighbor's name just two doors down. There's great personal privacy and freedom in a backyard life. There's also a great sadness to it.

We once built our homes with front porches, and we used them. We were involved in the comings and goings of our neighbors. We greeted, acknowledged, and celebrated each other's existence—a true community. It was a messier time, a nosier time, a more caring time.

I remember a season when I was feeling particularly sorry for myself. Lonely. Single. A pretty bank teller smiled at me. No big thing. She probably smiled at every customer. She was probably married. It didn't matter. I felt noticed—celebrated—all because of the smile of a stranger.

Watching Griffin greet each passing neighbor stirred in me a longing for more of a front-yard sort of life. Griffin's smile brightened a lot of days and lifted a lot of spirits. I doubt Luci and I would have known half as many of our neighbors if Griffin wasn't there—an appreciative audience of one, waiting to applaud anyone willing to step out from behind the curtain.

Paws **for** Prayer

O Father, I've worn myself out trying to be noticed and have gone into hiding. Unlock the door, drag me out, and let me venture forth, not to be noticed but to notice. Amen.

Truly I say to you, to the

extent that you did it to one

of these brothers of Mine,

even the least of them, you

did it to Me.

Matthew 25:40

Mutterings

The deepest principle in human nature is the craving to be appreciated.

—William James

Buck

Born to Run

The Haglunds are good, honest, trustworthy folks—lifelong friends. But when they started telling Buck stories, I had my doubts. Whoever heard of a dog who runs around the backyard gathering speed only to throw himself on his back so he can slide several yards just for the sheer joy of it?

No one is really sure what Buck is. His black tongue and coloring suggest a bit of Chow in his bloodline. He is sixty pounds of muscle that could easily be imagined hunting gazelle on the wild pampas. However, Buck doesn't live in Africa. He lives directly across the street with the Haglunds.

When Ryan and Jason told me how their dad "walked" Buck, I had to see for myself. It turns out you need a car to walk Buck. Find a deserted stretch of highway. Roll down the windows. Get out of the way. On command, Buck glides from the backseat, through the open front window, and onto the grassy strip along the side of the road.

Then you take the car up to twenty-five or thirty miles an hour, and Buck begins to lengthen his stride as he paces the car, running up and down the grassy bank. A friend of mine once

Something to ◆ Chew on

If we all ran at the same pace, we'd always be in each other's way.

144

◆ ◆ ◆ ◆ ◆ ◆ ◆ ◆ ◆ ◆ ◆ ◆ ◆ ◆ ◆

quipped, "Some bodies are made for speed, others for comfort." No question which category Buck fits into.

We drove for a couple of miles before stopping long enough for Buck to attack a water sprinkler for a drink. We were still only halfway through his walk. The drive back was Buck's cool-down period. We drove only fifteen to twenty miles an hour while Buck effortlessly kept pace.

The first time Tom brought Buck over to meet Griffin, I was a bit concerned. Griff would have been little more than a snack for Buck. Fortunately, Buck and Griffin became sniffin' buddies. It's kind of nice having such a powerful friend close by.

I tend to compare other dogs to the one in our home. I'm so used to Griffin's little shuffle walk that any dog looks quick and agile in comparison. But Buck is truly in a class by himself—born to run.

◆ ◆ ◆ ◆ ◆ ◆ ◆ ◆ ◆ ◆ ◆ ◆ ◆ ◆ ◆

Paws **for** Prayer

*Loving Creator, thank you that I'm not in
competition with anyone for your love and
attention. Amen.*

But to each one is given the

manifestation of the Spirit

for the common good.

1 Corinthians 12:7

Mutterings

God ... made me fast!
And when I run, I feel
his pleasure.

—Eric Liddell

The Fireplace Romantic

Never Pick Your Dog over Your Wife

It was one of those romantic evenings. A soft glow from the fireplace played across Luci's face. Her eyes sparkled. We enjoyed a quiet dinner in the living room. The pace of life had finally slowed to the point that the activities of the day were just a distant memory.

"Let's sit by the fire for a while," she whispered.

Fireplaces are magical.

Luci had arranged the pillows in front of the fire. Two mugs of hot chocolate sat on the hearth.

"Talk to me," she said.

What more could you want? Only one thing to my way of thinking.

"Griff! Come join us by the fire," I said.

Griffin roused himself from his spot by the door and soon settled between Luci and me in front of the fire. I noticed the sparkle in Luci's eye was gone. Not a good sign. Immediately, I played back the last few moments. No, nothing there to suggest a problem.

"Can't you just sit and talk with me? I didn't want to share this moment with our dog. Please don't use Griffin as a buffer between us."

Something to ♥ Chew on

If your closest friend is a pet, better check to see if you're a chicken.

148

Too close! Too intimate! I'm a romantic at a distance. It's not all that safe up close. I still need a crutch, or a puppy, for protection like the child hugging his favorite stuffed animal for security. I just picked my dog over my wife!

It pretty much botched the rest of the evening, nursing my male ego and defending a romantic image that only existed in my head. I guess I wasn't the romantic I thought.

Never Pick Your Dog over Your Wife

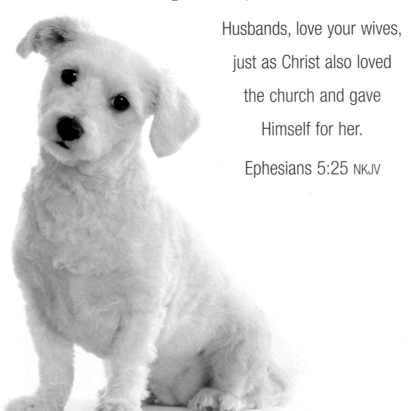

Paws for Prayer

O Father God, I thought we'd covered this!
I don't want to live my life inside my head.
Awaken my heart that my love might be
tangible and present. Amen.

Husbands, love your wives,

just as Christ also loved

the church and gave

Himself for her.

Ephesians 5:25 NKJV

Mutterings

When a man's best friend
is his dog, that dog has a
problem.

—Edward Abbey

Sneakin' Up on Griffin

Sounds of Home

I snuck up on Griffin today.

There was a time when that would have been all but impossible. A young Golden Labrador can pick out the slightest scraping sound of a Milk Bone being drawn from the box in another room while the television is blaring. But Griffin is an old dog. His face is gray, his joints are stiff, and his sleep is filled with the silent peace that comes to those who are dull of hearing.

I snuck up on Griffin today.

I watched him breathe, his belly going up and down—much the way a baby's does. Sometime during the night, he'd moved from his proper bed on the floor to the forbidden territory of the living-room couch. I laid a hand on his side, and he slept on. Finally, the warmth of my touch drew him from his slumber.

I suppose the ritual of waking up is a daily commentary on life. Does consciousness flood slumber at the slight click that comes the moment before the alarm rings? Or does it come in stages? Toes curl, legs stretch, eyes are rubbed, the swallow reflex tested?

Sounds of Home

Waking up puts dreams on hold, unravels the cocoon of conscious isolation, and opens the possibility of embracing another of God's creatures.

I snuck up on Griffin today.

The first part of Griffin to awaken was his tail. Long before he opened his eyes, long before he stretched old limbs or scratched new itches, he wagged his tail 180 beats to the minute. The rhythmic sound of Griffin's joy was like a calm hand on my own heart. What trust resides in that old dog! No need to check the hand on his side, no resentment at being awakened, only the "peaceful, easy feeling" of conscious companionship.

I snuck up on Griffin today.

He greeted me with the sounds of home.

Paws **for** Prayer

Prince of Peace, sneak up on me and
awaken my heart. Amen.

For He gives to His beloved

even in his sleep.

Psalm 127:2

Mutterings

I sleep … but my heart is awake.

—Gerald May

Falling Short

Saying Good-bye a Little Bit Each Day

Griffin didn't make it today. He didn't make it yesterday either. It's been coming for sometime now, but I didn't allow myself to think about it. Hip dysplasia has been part of our working vocabulary with Griffin since he was a pup. Where other Labs can turn on a dime, Griff overshoots by a mile. Where other Labs leap, Griffin has this little hop. Where other Labs have full flanks of muscle on their hindquarters, Griffin has chicken legs.

Luci wasn't feeling well this morning, and Griffin tried to join her in bed. He took a couple of steps and belly flopped against the edge of the bed, hind legs kicking pathetically, trying to gain some purchase. I gathered him in my arms and helped him up. He didn't seem embarrassed at his obvious failure. He just tucked himself into the curve of Luci's blanket covered leg, happy to be near her. I rubbed his ear for a long time. He's saying good-bye a little bit each day. Now that I think about it, our trips around the park are growing shorter—two laps is pretty much his limit. How gracefully Griffin lets go of this life, with no resentment or remonstrations. He doesn't swim upstream. His is an accepting

■ ■ ■ ■ ■ ■ ■ ■ ■ ■ ■ ■ ■ ■ ■ ■ ■ ■

heart content with who he is today. Oh, to be so accepting of my journey through life with my retreating hairline, bum knee, and astigmatism.

Paws **for** Prayer

Father God, Daddy, I don't much mind a wrinkled face and hands; it's a wrinkled heart that scares me. Please keep young what counts, and let the rest grow old gracefully. Amen.

Even to your old age I will be the same, and even to your graying years I will bear you! I have done it, and I will carry you; and I will bear you and I will deliver you.

Isaiah 46:4

Mutterings

God gives us bodies
that wear out so we can
go home.

—My Mom

Almost Good-bye

Enjoying the Time Left

Something to ◆ Chew on

When you start missing what isn't gone, you stop enjoying what's left.

Griffin slept in today. He wasn't up for much of a walk. He stuck close, head down. Once around the park was all he could handle. He looked like he'd just finished a trek across the Himalayas. Half a dozen steps into the house, he was down and out. No classic spin to mark his spot to snooze. He just plopped. Too pooped.

He failed to greet me at the door after I'd been out. Everything about his face had sagged overnight. We were at the vet a few weeks back. Everything had been normal. This wasn't normal.

I called the vet. "Come now. We'll work you in."

A couple of hours later, the vet took me into a side room to explain Griff's situation. He showed me his X-rays and tried to explain to me what a dense cell count meant.

"He's very anemic. He's lost some weight since we saw him last month. His blood count is way down. His lethargy could be from hip pain, or perhaps he's bleeding internally. His spleen is starting to look suspicious."

He was saying good-bye.

She suggested an ultrasound for the spleen, biopsy work, and

160

the possibility of major surgery. I promised Griff after his last bit of surgery that I wouldn't put him through it again. I wouldn't put myself through it either.

"With a big dog, it is usually the frame that wears out first. You probably need to just focus on easing his discomfort as much as possible." Her voice started to sound as if it were coming from an echo chamber.

"Thank you for checking Griff out. Twelve is pretty old for a big dog, isn't it?"

"Yes."

I couldn't make out what she was saying. It was just sound. My chest was tight. I wouldn't cry. Not there. Not then. I wondered if I could make it home? What would I say to Luci?

Griffin shuffled out the clinic's door. I lifted him into the front seat like a limp doll.

I missed him already.

They gave him a steroid injection to ease his pain. What was I to take for my pain?

I came home with an arsenal of pills, double-strength Cosequin, Rimadyl, and vitamins. These pills weren't for a season; they are to be

◆ ◆ ◆ ◆ ◆ ◆ ◆ ◆ ◆ ◆ ◆ ◆ ◆ ◆ ◆

taken for the rest of his life.

I held him for a long time once we got home. Luci and I cried together. We gave him back to God again.

Two days later, Griffin seems like his old self. He wants to walk. His ears are up. He greets us at the door, his tail wagging … a reprieve.

Paws **for** Prayer

Lord God, Truth and Life, let me savor the moments and not fret the what-ifs and might-have-beens. Amen.

And who of you by being worried can add a single hour to his life?

Matthew 6:27

Mutterings

The evening of a well-
spent life brings its lamps
with it.

—Joseph Joubert

The Best Howler in the Neighborhood

Ginger the Diva

Something to ♥ Chew on

Don't swallow the range of your emotions out of concern for what others might think.

I've never owned a truly great howler. A whimperer, barker, and mumbler, yes. A great howler, no. Griffin has blessed us with less than a dozen true howls in his entire lifetime: short-lived, of medium range and volume, infrequent, with little sense of occasion. At best, Griffin is a blues singer of average ability.

Luci and I have never been able to isolate the necessary variables that trigger Griffin's howl. We do know that the upper register of Luci's violin and a sense of privacy are key elements. Griffin can't howl if he knows there is an audience. Technically, this is known as "shy-howler syndrome."

However, there is one pup in the neighborhood that suffers from none of Griffin's ineptitudes or inhibitions. She's a howler of extraordinary giftedness. An artist. A diva. Ginger has it all: a Siberian Husky, beautifully colored, smooth as silk. She is pretty enough to make you want to go right out and get one of your own.

Ginger lives across the street with the Snyders. If you're lucky, you can catch Ginger in a melancholy mood when the stars are out and so are the Snyders. From her backyard, she holds court, the neighborhood in the pad of her paw. Her stamina, frequency, volume, and sense of occasion are exceptional. But it is her range of emotional expression and color that truly sets her apart.

The Snyders once tried to apologize for one of Ginger's backyard concerts. They might as well have tried to apologize for Mona Lisa's smile, or the 1812 Overture. Ginger's hallowed howls are magical enough to cause favorite television shows to go unwatched, cut short phone calls back home, and draw folks from the warmth of their homes just to bask in the wonder and awe of it all.

If Ginger were a singer, she'd sing arias.

Ginger the Diva

♥ ♥ ♥ ♥ ♥ ♥ ♥ ♥ ♥ ♥ ♥ ♥ ♥ ♥ ♥

Paws for Prayer

Dear God, Singer of Great Songs, the critics still intimidate me, and I often swallow what I ought to share. Can you help me? I'm having trouble believing that my songs are worth singing. Amen.

Sing to Him a new song;

play skillfully with a

shout of joy.

Psalm 33:3 NKJV

Mutterings

The average person goes to
his grave with his music
still in him.

—Oliver Wendell Holmes

"Ai Luv Oo"

Actions Speak Louder Than Words

Ginger has another talent—she talks. Not "bark, bark," but words you can understand, like the Scooby-Doo of cartoon fame. Catch Ginger in the right mood, and you will likely hear, "Mama," or "Ai luv oo."

Ginger's articulations of affection are clearer than some I've heard from human throats, including mine. It was a real shock the first time I heard her. I didn't know it was even possible. I wondered if Ginger really knew what she was saying. Wondered if most of us know when we mouth those same words.

Ginger's verbal response is prompted by encouragement, the desire for praise, and a hoped-for treat. Perhaps she's not all that different from the rest of us.

"I love you." Three syllables, eight letters: a subject, verb, and object—the simplest of sentences. Yet, it is the most complex statement in all the world.

The motive behind the words is more important than the words themselves. "I love you" can quickly become a parrotlike response with no conscious thought or genuine emotion behind it. "I love you" can be a terrifying declaration coming from the wrong lips.

Something to ● Chew on

"I love you" means little if there is no wag, nuzzle, or lick to go with it.

168

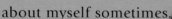

Those words can bind us together whether we like it or not. Sometimes we don't like it one bit. Other times, we think we'll die if we don't hear them soon.

Ginger shows her affection the same way all dogs do. She wags, nuzzles, and licks. She also happens to talk. I wonder which one of those communicates the most love? Ginger's speech is a learned response, an amazing trick. Her other loving ways weren't taught to her at all. She doesn't even think about them. They just happen. She can't help herself.

When I say to Luci, "I love you," she usually responds, "How do you know?" How do I know? How come she's not satisfied with my simple declaration of love? Doesn't seem a fair question! She wants more? Well … yes. And she deserves more.

In matters of love, Luci is way smarter than Ginger. I'm not so sure about myself sometimes.

Actions Speak Louder Than Words

Paws **for** Prayer

*Gentle Physician, I say an awful lot of the right words
without managing to convey the right message. Is there
some surgery that would help me to speak from my heart?
If so, I'd like to schedule an appointment. Amen.*

Let us not love with word

or with tongue, but in deed

and truth.

1 John 3:18

Mutterings

The way to love someone is to
lightly run your finger over that
person's soul until you find
a crack, and then gently
pour your love into
that crack.

—Keith Miller

Packing

Part of the Family

The movers came yesterday.

Griffin watched two strangers take everything that was familiar out of his house. He greeted each one at the door with a friendly wag, but watched them closely. "Don't forget me!"

Griffin, I hate the thought of being left too.

I found Griffin in the bathroom, using one of my old tennis shoes for a pillow. Softly snoring, he didn't look comfortable. His neck was cocked at an awkward angle, trying to conform to the shape of my shoe. He doesn't want to be left, so he attaches himself to something he figures we're taking along.

I attach myself to all sorts of things too, in the attempt to make myself more acceptable—degrees, clothes, conduct.

Griffin, you're worth far more than what you've attached yourself to.

Our house has become Grand Central Station. The neighborhood kids are in and out all the time now. "Why ya movin'?" "Is Griffin going with you?" "Where are you going?" Same questions over and over.

Griffin has brought me his leash at least six times today. I suspect

172

it's more complicated than merely wanting to go for a walk. He wants to assure himself of our relationship. *Griff, the leash proves little. You are far more than just a walking companion.*

Wise neighbors have come to help. They've moved before. They know it takes longer than you think. They know how hard it is to let go of the things that house so many memories.

Griffin, you are more than just a memory.

The house looks small without furniture. The worn light-brown carpet is all that's left besides Griffin. He's doing his best Manatee imitation, the blob at one with the carpet, guarding the door to the garage.

Griffin, you're much more valuable than what comes and goes from our home. You are a doorway into our hearts. You are part of our family.

Part of the Family

Paws for Prayer

Lord God, how silly to think you'd ever forget me! Now if you could just help me with the crick in my neck…. Amen.

I go to prepare a place for you. And if I go and prepare a place for you, I will come again and receive you to Myself; that where I am, *there* you may be also.

John 14:2–3 NKJV

Mutterings

They say three moves is
equal to one fire. Every
so often, "they" are right.

—Anonymous

The Art of Waiting

Hurry Up and Wait

Something to ◆ Chew on

Waiting isn't being put on hold. Waiting is a matter of taking hold.

How do you feel about waiting? Is it one of your favorite activities or more like sitting in the dentist chair waiting for the Novocain to take effect? Ever watch a dog in wait mode? It's pretty much what dogs do. They wait for you to get up. They wait to be let out. They wait to go for a walk. They wait to be fed. They wait for you to come home. They wait.

Waiting takes on the appearance of rapt attention at mealtime at our house. Every gesture and nuance is studied in great detail and interpreted as "Let's give Old Griffin a treat, what say?" At which point, Griff works his patented head tilt to perfection, usually resulting in a bit of toast moving from the table to his mouth.

Griffin is a serious student of Luci's and my habits and routines. Donning a jacket or pair of sunglasses suggests a trip outside and a possible walk in the park: Griff front and center. Tail wagging. Head tilt flawlessly executed. We even have to be careful what we say and the inflection we use. Even spelling w-a-l-k can send Griffin in search of his l-e-a-s-h.

Last night, there was a big storm with lightning and thunder— rare occurrences in Southern California, not so rare in our new

176

◆ ◆ ◆ ◆ ◆ ◆ ◆ ◆ ◆ ◆ ◆ ◆ ◆ ◆ ◆

home state of New York. I went downstairs to check on Griffin. I didn't make a sound. Still, he was sitting there looking straight at me as I rounded the corner.

"Fully expected you to see how I'm doing," he seemed to say. He waits. We sat there by the floor-to-ceiling window and watched the sky sing and dance—nothing like a puppy in a storm.

I've learned a lot about waiting from Griffin. He's a good model for one so poor at the art. I used to think waiting was pretty much the same as killing time; slow stagnation; forced, delayed gratification; enduring the slowness of others; a waste of time. I have a different take now.

Waiting is an active exercise of hope, born of careful observation over time, that produces a deep understanding of who or what is being waited for. Waiting is a skill well worth developing. Few things offer such attractive rewards as waiting.

"Yet those who wait for the LORD
Will gain new strength;
They will mount up with wings like eagles,
They will run and not get tired,
They will walk and not become weary."
—Isaiah 40:31

Hurry Up and Wait

Paws **for** Prayer

Father, Patient One, you know how hard it is for me to wait. Instant solutions and success are what I usually crave. Season my soul that I might not miss eternity in the here and now. Amen.

Wait for the LORD; be

strong, and let your heart

take courage; yea, wait for

the LORD!

Psalm 27:14 RSV

 *Mutterings*

Don't accept your dog's admiration as conclusive evidence that you are wonderful.

—Ann Landers

A Hard Pill to Swallow

Grin and Bear It

I found one of Griff's green and white Cosequin pills on the deck this morning. I thought he swallowed it last night. He must have held it in his mouth until I wasn't looking and then spit it out.

Griffin is not a stranger to the rituals of pill taking. Allergy season and pill season go together. But now every day is pill day. Two Cosequin and half a Rimadyl morning and night.

Griffin accepts this new arrangement with his own blend of resignation and resistance. He comes when I call, sits when I ask, and sniffs expectantly. Then as I set out my arsenal of pills, Griff's ears drop and his jaw tightens.

"Open your mouth, Griffin."

Teeth still clinched, he doesn't try to get away. He's just not going to cooperate at the level of voluntarily taking his medicine. I pry open his mouth and slide the pills to the back of his throat.

"There! That wasn't so bad."

Tail wags. It's over. No more pills until evening.

I don't suppose we're required to like everything we have to

180

swallow. Vegetables will never taste as good as candy, and taking out the trash is never as much fun as going out for a treat. But a healthy life often embraces the unpleasant for its own good. Griffin may not wag his tail, but he doesn't tuck his tail and run either. He may tighten his jaw, but he never tightens his heart.

♥ ♥ ♥ ♥ ♥ ♥ ♥ ♥ ♥ ♥ ♥ ♥ ♥ ♥ ♥

Paws **for** Prayer

Dear Father, I'm so thankful that you haven't been angry with this child for nearly two thousand years. Amen.

[God] disciplines us for our

good, so that we may share

His holiness.

Hebrews 12:10

 *Mutterings*

It is only by obedience
that we understand the
teaching of God.

—Oswald Chambers

Old Yeller

Star Is Born

Something to ● Chew on

Christ-figures are common in stories but uncommon in real life. There's only One.

Long before Griffin's brief debut as Old Yeller in a Disney promo, I was marked by the story of Old Yeller. Most folks think Old Yeller was a Golden Labrador. No doubt he had a lot of Lab in him, but the Old Yeller lineage is a bit more complicated than that.

Had it been just a story about the adventures of a boy and his dog, it would have been little more than a couple of hours of distraction. The death of Old Yeller and the way he died marked it as a classic for all time.

The final scenes still touch me: Yeller fighting off the rabid wolf near the campfire; the days of uncertainty over Yeller's wounds; his developing rabies; and his death at the hands of the boy. This piece of fiction parallels another story that really happened.

Perhaps you've lost your place in that story due to the cultural trappings that often surround it. Perhaps you've never really known where you fit in. I still remember watching a Russian Orthodox priest viewing the crucifixion scene in the *Jesus* film for the first time. He wept. I guess it just hit him at a new level.

The laying down of a life for another.

Taking on the sickness that plagues the world.

Death at the hands of the very ones He came to save.

A wholehearted love that never stops giving.

Maybe you think I'm wrong to make the comparison. Maybe not.

When's the last time you revisited the story of Jesus? It is worth another look. It is worth more than a look.

If you ever wonder whatever happened to the original Old Yeller of the movie (his real name was Spike), he lived several more years on a ranch several miles north of Hollywood and died at a ripe old age. If you wonder whatever happened to Jesus Christ, he rose from the dead and he lives today. He's prepared a place for you, and he longs for you to come home.

Star Is Born

● ● ● ● ● ● ● ● ● ● ● ● ● ● ●

Paws for Prayer

Dear Lord, thank you. Thank you.
Thank you. Amen.

For one will hardly die for a
righteous man; though
perhaps for the good man
someone would dare even
to die. But God
demonstrates His own love
toward us, in that while we
were yet sinners, Christ died
for us.

Romans 5:7–8

Mutterings

Belief is truth held
in the mind; faith is a
fire in the heart.

—Joseph Fort Newton

A Tail-Wagging Reunion

Dear Griffin ...

Something to ■ Chew on

Good-bye isn't necessarily the end of the story, but it does mean a chapter has ended and another begun.

This wasn't how it was supposed to end. Luci and I are half a world away from you. Our trip to Malaysia cost more than I would have spent: a last moment with you. Of course, that's foolishness. We said good-bye the way we always say good-bye. You staggered over and put your head between my legs so that I could rub your ears. I hurried off to catch a plane and pushed from my mind the possibility that I would never see you again. Wish I'd lingered a moment longer.

Our friends Gene and Betty e-mailed that you had another stroke … couldn't move. Your heart was still strong, but your body had worn out. It was time to let go—you were already gone. Luci and I cried under the stars of Malaysia and gave you back to the Giver of all good gifts.

The next morning I was greeted with the lingering remnants of a dream about you....

We were in a high mountain meadow. You were in your prime. Your hips were perfect, and you ran. Oh, how you ran! Like lightning darting here and there full of the joy of doing what you were

Dear Griffin ...

■ ■ ■ ■ ■ ■ ■ ■ ■ ■ ■ ■ ■ ■ ■ ■

created to do. And jump! Griffin, you who never got so much as three inches off the ground now leaped higher than my head.

I was standing with my back to a high cliff, and you came up to me and did what you could never do. You reared up on your back legs, put your paws on my shoulders, and looked into my eyes with a searching look full of understanding and love. Then your gaze turned playful. You let your full weight push against my shoulders, and we fell backwards off the cliff.

I noticed for the first time that it was a waterfall. We laughed and laughed as we tumbled together through impossible heights and into a deep pool. And underwater we continued to laugh—no danger here, no fear, only the exuberant thrill of life and wholeness neither of us could ever know this side of Eternity.

I lay there in bed and smiled through the tears as a comforting peace settled in my heart. The One who gave you to us is holding me now, and I think he is holding you, too. Luci was right—the joy of knowing you far outweighs the pain of saying good-bye. We miss you, Griffin.

Scout out the best walks for us, but forget the leash. We won't need it there. I'll see you soon.

Gary

Was the dream a glimpse into the next life or a gift of comfort from the Great Comforter himself? I don't know about the first; I am sure of the second.

Will our pets be with us in heaven? Biblically there is no direct answer to that question. Still, I think the Bible may tilt in favor of a future similar to my dream. God certainly cares about the animals of this world (Jonah 4:11; Matthew 6:26). We know there will be animals in heaven (Isaiah 65:25). And then there is the curious way our pets are humanized and enfolded into our families. Love is stronger than death. Perhaps that "enfolding" extends beyond the grave and into our heavenly family.

C. S. Lewis and John Wesley, two of the world's greatest detectives of the faith, found similar reasons to hope for a heavenly tail-wagging reunion. Of course, if you hope to see your pets in heaven, the most important thing is to make sure you're going there.

Paws **for** Prayer

Father, thank you for reminding me that no matter how deep the sorrow, the wound, or the loss—there is a comfort deeper still. Amen.

And He will wipe away every tear from their eyes; and there will no longer be any death; there will no longer be any mourning, or crying, or pain.

Revelation 21:4

Mutterings

The most important thing
to know about
heaven is how to get there.

—Peter Kreeft

Additional copies of *What My Dog Taught Me about Life*
are available wherever good books are sold.

If you have enjoyed this book, or if it has had an impact on your life,
we would like to hear from you.

Please contact us at

HONOR BOOKS
Cook Communications Ministries, Dept. 201
4050 Lee Vance View
Colorado Springs, CO 80918

Or visit our Web site

www.cookministries.com

HONOR ⊞ BOOKS
Inspiration and Motivation for the Seasons of Life